HAMPTON-BROWN
HIGH POINT

SUCCESS IN LANGUAGE • LITERATURE • CONTENT

Practice Book

LEVEL C

HAMPTON-BROWN

Practice Book Contents

UNIT 1 MIND MAP

Personal Expression

DIRECTIONS Use the mind map to show your ideas about personal expression and creativity. As you read the selections in the unit, add new ideas you learn to the map.

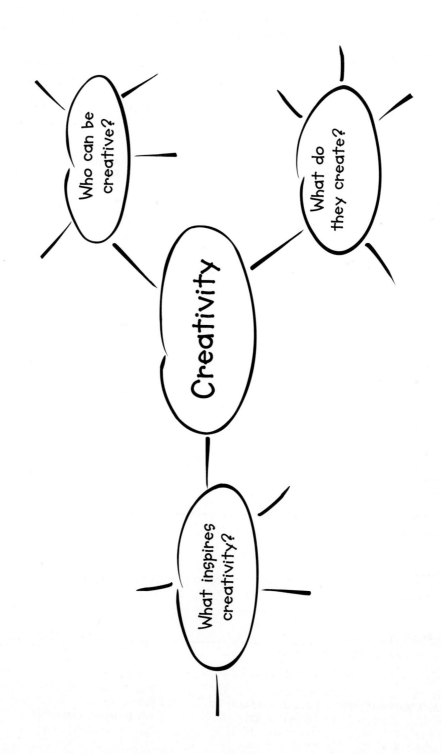

Who can be creative?

What do they create?

Creativity

What inspires creativity?

BUILD LANGUAGE AND VOCABULARY

Describe a Work of Art

DIRECTIONS Read each sentence. Draw a line to a phrase that adds more information to the sentence. Read the new sentence to a partner.

Phrases

1. Nam June Paik is a
   video artist _____ .

   growing up in Korea

2. Even as a child _____
   Paik had unusual ideas.

   in the 1990s

3. Most of the works
   Paik created _____
   involve television sets.

   with amazing talents

4. *TV Cello* is a famous
   piece of art created _____ .

   stacked in the shape
   of a cello

5. Three TVs _____
   play music in this piece.

   by Nam June Paik

Complete Sentences

A **complete sentence** has a subject and a predicate.

A video artist creates images.
  subject   predicate

A **phrase** is a group of words without a subject and a predicate.

  with video technology

Add a **phrase** to a complete sentence to give more information.

A video artist creates images
      complete sentence
with video technology.
        phrase

![TV Cello sculpture]

TV Cello, Nam June Paik, mixed media. Copyright ©1971.

DIRECTIONS Study the picture. Add a phrase to expand each sentence.

6. A stool stands behind the TV cello
   _____ .

7. Wires curl _____

   _____ .

8. Paik stacked the TVs _____ .

9. There are plastic boxes _____ .

10. The TVs display images _____ .

Theater Words

New Words

accept the challenge

brilliant idea

concept

creative

musical

personal touch

realize a vision

represent

stage play

talented

Relate Words

DIRECTIONS Work with a group. Write the new words where they belong in the chart.

Words About an Artist	Words About a Performance
creative	musical

Use Context Clues

DIRECTIONS Read the paragraph. Replace each bold word with the correct new word.

Our teacher had a ____brilliant idea____: we would
                    1. clever plan

sing and dance in a _____ about our school.
                    2. performance

Her _____ was that we would think of a
        3. idea

_____ way to tell about being a student at our
    4. imaginative

school. Our class decided to _____, and we started
                            5. try it

writing! Since none of us are _____ artists, the art
                            6. gifted

teacher offered to design sets that _____ our
                                    7. stand for

school classrooms and hallways. Our drama teacher was excited to

_____.
    8. see her plan become a reality

Use Descriptive Language

DIRECTIONS Work with a partner to finish the chart. Picture each subject in your mind. Write details to describe it. Then compare the subject to something else.

> ### Descriptive Language
> **Descriptive language** uses specific words, sensory details, and comparisons to help the reader "see" an event or scene.
>
> The long scaly tail of the alligator glistened
> <u>sensory detail</u>   <u>specific verb</u>
> like a jewel in the Amazon rain forest.
> <u>comparison</u>   <u>specific noun</u>

Subject	Descriptive Words	Comparisons
vines	climbers, explorers, encircle, creep	like hungry snakes, like curious explorers
lion		
birds		
trees		

DIRECTIONS Write a paragraph about a jungle. Describe the vines, lions, birds, and trees. Use details from your chart.

_____

_____

_____

_____

_____

Name _____   Date _____

Relate Main Idea and Details

DIRECTIONS Read the article Rafael wrote for his school newspaper. Then complete the main idea and details chart.

A Great Stage Show!

The Lion King was much better as a stage play than as a movie. Seeing the live production was an experience I won't forget.

When you see real actors dressed in elaborate costumes, it really captures your imagination. A movie just can't match that. Julie Taymor, who has worked on other Broadway productions, was the main designer. She and her team did a great job creating the amazing costumes.

The sets and the lighting were also wonderful. I thought the atmosphere of Africa was better in the stage play than in the movie. There were some great special effects, too. For instance, when the lake dried up, I had to remind myself that it was a trick of the eye.

Seeing the actors in person, instead of on a movie screen, was thrilling. Watching them on stage, I really thought they were jungle creatures. They trotted, slithered, and glided across the stage like real-life animals.

The costumes, the sets, the lighting, and the performances made the stage play great. It was more exciting than any movie I have ever seen.

Main Idea and Details Chart

Main Idea:

Detail:

Detail:

Detail:

DIRECTIONS Write a summary of the article. Use information from the chart.

_____
_____
_____
_____

© Hampton-Brown

GRAMMAR: COMPLETE SENTENCES

A Brilliant Idea from Bali

DIRECTIONS Read each sentence. Draw one line under the simple subject. Draw two lines under the simple predicate.

Subjects and Predicates

A complete sentence has a subject and a predicate. The **simple subject** is the noun or pronoun the sentence is about.

The leather **puppets** prance across the screen.

The **simple predicate** is the verb that tells what the subject is, does, or has. It agrees in number with the subject.

The puppets **delight** the audience.

1. In 1975, <u>Julie Taymor</u> <u><u>traveled</u></u> throughout Indonesia.

2. In Indonesia, she encountered Balinese puppetry.

3. This ancient form of art sparked ideas in Taymor's mind.

4. Balinese puppets are either flat or three-dimensional.

5. In Indonesia, puppeteers use the puppets in two main ways.

6. Artists use the flat puppets in shadow plays.

7. A shadow artist holds the carved, leather puppets between a lamp and a screen.

8. The flat puppets cast shadows on the screen.

9. The artist performs the speech, songs, and sound effects for the scenes.

10. In daylight, puppeteers use the other kind of puppet.

11. They manipulate three-dimensional puppets without a screen.

12. Julie Taymor probably watched both kinds of performances.

13. However, *The Lion King* reveals the influence of a third kind of Indonesian drama.

14. In this third form of drama, human dancers take the parts of the puppets.

15. They tell the story as puppets.

16. Taymor's costumes for *The Lion King* show the influence of this Indonesian form.

MORE ABOUT SUBJECTS AND PREDICATES Write a description of the flat shadow puppet shown on this page. Use words that help your description come to life. Draw a line under the simple subject in each sentence. Draw two lines under the simple predicate.

Balinese puppeteers cast shadows on a screen by holding flat puppets like this between a lamp and a screen.

WRITING: A MAIN IDEA PARAGRAPH

At the Theater

DIRECTIONS Talk about the theater or a
live performance with your group. What
happens during a performance? What is it
like? Write a paragraph about the theater.

Paragraph

A **paragraph** is a group
of sentences that all tell
about the same idea.

• A paragraph has a
  topic sentence that
  tells the main idea.

• It has **supporting
  details** that tell more
  about the main idea.

Write a **topic sentence**
to tell your main idea.
Tell what you like
about the theater.
You might want to
write your topic
sentence at the end.
If so, begin the
paragraph with
your details.

_____

_____

_____

_____

_____

_____

Write **supporting
details** that give more
information about
your main idea. Give
specific examples of
what you like or
describe how your
favorite performance
looks or sounds.

_____

_____

_____

_____

_____

_____

_____

_____

_____

_____

_____

Write a **concluding
sentence**. Sum up
your ideas. Remind
your readers about
the main idea.

_____

_____

The Lion King Goes to Broadway
LEVEL C TE page T25

7

Calculate Costs of a Production

DIRECTIONS Work with a group. Arrange to interview the business manager of a community theater or school drama department.

1 Prepare your questions. Write them on the chart below.

2 Conduct the interview by phone, e-mail, or in person.
Ask your questions and write the answers.

Name of the Show: _____

Item	Costs	Income
Tickets How much income did you earn from ticket sales?		$
Salaries	$	
Advertising	$	$
Refreshments	$	$
Costumes, Props, Supplies, and Other Expenses	$	
Totals:	$	$

Be sure to ask about both costs and income.

3 Figure out the amount of profit or loss.

Total Income – Total Costs = $ _____ profit

or

Total Costs – Total Income = $ _____ loss

4 In your group, discuss how the theater should spend the profits or what should be done about the loss. Share your ideas with the class.

Words About Creativity

DIRECTIONS Create a word web for each new word.

Word: style
Example: how you wear your hair
Sentence: He has an unusual style for shooting baskets.

1.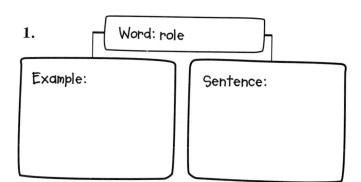
Word: role
Example:
Sentence:

5.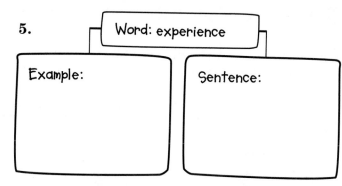
Word: experience
Example:
Sentence:

2.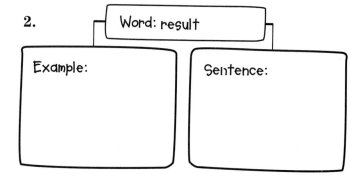
Word: result
Example:
Sentence:

6.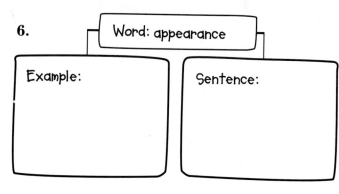
Word: appearance
Example:
Sentence:

3.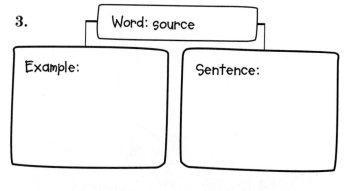
Word: source
Example:
Sentence:

7.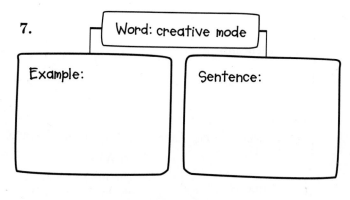
Word: creative mode
Example:
Sentence:

4.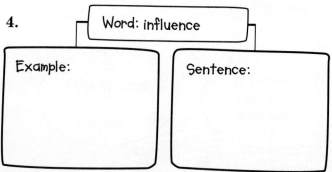
Word: influence
Example:
Sentence:

8.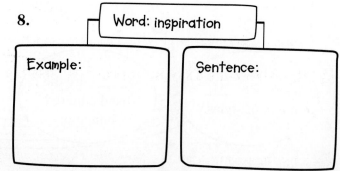
Word: inspiration
Example:
Sentence:

GRAMMAR: SUBJECT-VERB AGREEMENT

The Music Game

Start

This game __is__ about a great musician.

My favorite singer _____ born in 1975.

Subject-Verb Agreement

Forms of the verb **be** must agree with the subject. One person or thing takes the **singular** form: **am**, **is**, or **was.**

The **song is** great.

More than one takes the **plural** form: **are** or **were**.

The **singers are** famous.

Now, even the band members _____ stars!

He _____ from Arizona.

At first, he _____ a solo artist.

His records _____ big sellers.

His first songs _____ rock and roll songs.

How to Play
The Music Game

1. Play in a group of three. One person is the "manager." The other two are players.

2. Players each choose a game piece. Youngest player goes first.

3. When it's your turn, roll the die to get started. Go forward that many spaces.

4. Read aloud the sentence in the space you land on. Then choose a form of the verb *be* to complete it.

5. Move ahead one space for each letter of a correct verb. (**Example:** For *was*, move ahead 3 spaces.) Go back one space for an incorrect verb. "Manager" determines accuracy.

I _____ his biggest fan.

Later, he _____ in a band.

He _____ very famous.

To Win

The first player to go around the board two times wins.

His first drummer _____ Mexican American.

Today, his music _____ a mix of styles.

I _____ sure the band admired him, too.

They _____ people he admired.

His guitar players _____ Native Americans.

10

© Hampton-Brown

Concert of the Year!

DIRECTIONS Read each sentence. Draw one line under the simple subject. Draw two lines under the simple predicate.

1. The <u>concert</u> of the year <u><u>begins</u></u> in ten minutes.

2. Young people all over the state enjoy this band.

3. The excited fans fill every seat in the auditorium.

4. A curtain of purple velvet slowly rises.

5. The audience sees a stage full of instruments.

6. In the middle of the stage stand the gleaming drums.

7. Behind the drums sits a long-haired drummer.

8. The drummer begins a low drum roll.

9. In come the other musicians!

10. Finally, the singer struts onto the stage to a round of applause.

11. There is excitement in the air.

12. The talented and well-loved lead vocalist sings.

> ### Subjects and Predicates
> The **simple subject** is the most important word in the subject. The **simple predicate** is the most important word in the predicate.
>
> The popular <u>singer</u> <u><u>runs</u></u> on stage.
>   subject   predicate
>
> In some sentences, the simple subject comes after the simple predicate.
>
> Here <u><u>comes</u></u> the lead <u>singer</u>.
>   simple   subject
>   predicate

DIRECTIONS In four of the sentences above, the subject comes after the verb. Rewrite each sentence. Put the subject before the verb.

13. The gleaming drums _____

_____ .

14. _____

_____

15. _____

_____

16. _____

_____

SUM IT UP

Classify and Evaluate Literature

DIRECTIONS Work with a partner. Brainstorm two new categories.
Complete the chart about "Inspiration."

Sources of Inspiration	Music-Related Job		
Mexican music tropical rhythms	singing radio jingles		
Summary: Tish Hinojosa was inspired by	Summary: During her career,	Summary:	Summary:

DIRECTIONS Complete the sentences to evaluate the interview.

1. The purpose of the interview was to

_____

_____ .

2. I think the author was interested in

_____

because she asked questions about

_____ .

3. I think the interview was well written because

_____

_____ .

4. If I could interview Hinojosa, I would ask:

_____

_____ .

At Home in One's Work

DIRECTIONS Work with a partner. Read each sentence and write the correct form of the verb.

1. Artists' homes _____influence_____ and
   _____ their work.
   <u>influence / influences</u>
   <u>inspire / inspires</u>

2. Both a painter and a photographer
   _____ ideas in nearby settings.
   <u>find / finds</u>

3. Sometimes, open plains or a snow-covered
   mountain _____ an idea.
   <u>spark / sparks</u>

4. R.C. Gorman _____ and
   _____the scenery around him.
   <u>see / sees</u>
   <u>paint / paints</u>

5. Desert colors and hues _____ in
   his paintings.
   <u>glow / glows</u>

6. Poets and songwriters _____
   images in their environments.
   <u>discover / discovers</u>

7. Joseph Bruchac _____ quiet and _____
   to his surroundings.
   <u>remain / remains</u>
   <u>listen / listens</u>

8. Tish Hinojosa's words and music _____ Southwestern.
   <u>sound / sounds</u>

9. An artist's ideas or point of view _____ reflected in the artwork.
   <u>is / are</u>

10. The artist's habitat or experiences _____ influences, too.
    <u>is / are</u>

Subject-Verb Agreement

A **compound subject** with **and** takes a **plural verb.**

The **artist and** the **painter decorate** the studio.

A compound subject with **or** takes a **verb** that agrees with the **last simple subject.**

Either the **artists or** their **gallery advertises** new work.

Both verbs in a **compound predicate** agree with the subject.

The gallery **sends** invitations and **prepares** refreshments.

Navajo Return, Lithograph by R. C. Gorman. Copyright © 1997

Parts of a Book

DIRECTIONS Tell where you can find each type of page in a book.
Write the purpose for each page.

1. Index

Ackerman, William, 65	Liszt, Franz, 33, 42, 49, 89
Bach, Johann Sebastian, 9, 13, 14–17,	Mendelssohn, Felix, 42
33, 45, 53, 81, 89	Mozart, Wolfgang Amadeus, 9, 18–23,
Beethoven, Ludwig van, 9, 24–29, 35,	25, 29, 33, 34, 35, 45, 50, 55, 76
52, 53, 73, 83, 89	Musgrave, Thea, 81
Bernstein, Leonard, 81	Prokofiev, Sergei, 9, 82–85
Boulanger, Lili, 79, 80, 81	Raposi, Joe, 81
Boulanger, Nadia, 9, 78–81	Reich, Steve, 65

back; gives page numbers where you can

find information about subjects

2. Glossary

ballet	an art form that uses dancing, music, and scenery to tell a story
cantata	a long, usually religious work for chorus and orchestra
concerto	a work in three movements for solo instrument(s) and orchestra
folk song	a traditional song, composer unknown, passed from one generation
	to the next
invention	short keyboard composition using melodies independent of each other
libretto	

3. Table of Contents

CONTENTS

INTRODUCTION • 9

THE RED PRIEST:
ANTONIO VIVALDI • 10

4. Copyright Page

Text copyright © 1993 by Kathleen Krull
Illustrations copyright © 1993 by Kathryn Hewitt

All rights reserved. No part of this publication may be reproduced or transmitted in any
form or by any means, electronic or mechanical, including photocopy,
recording, or any information storage and retrieval system,
without permission in writing from the publisher.

Requests for permission to make copies of any part of the work should be mailed to:
Permissions Department, Harcourt Brace & Company, 6277 Sea Harbor Drive,
Orlando, Florida 32887-6777.

5. Title Page

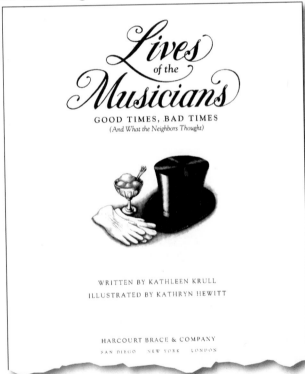

Lives
of the
Musicians

GOOD TIMES, BAD TIMES
(And What the Neighbors Thought)

WRITTEN BY KATHLEEN KRULL
ILLUSTRATED BY KATHRYN HEWITT

HARCOURT BRACE & COMPANY
SAN DIEGO   NEW YORK   LONDON

Using a Computer Catalog

Computer Catalog

A library's **computer catalog** is faster to use than a card catalog. You can search for a book by typing in an author's name, a book title, a subject, or a key word. Then you can print out the information and locate the book.

DIRECTIONS Answer the questions about using a computer catalog.

1. How is a computer catalog different from a card catalog?

_____

_____

_____

```
Welcome to the library!
       You may search
           A  AUTHOR
           T  TITLE
           Y  AUTHOR/TITLE SEARCH
           S  SUBJECT
           W  WORDS in title
           C  CALL No.
           P  Repeat PREVIOUS Search
Choose one (A, T, Y, S, W, C, P): S
```

2. What steps do you take to find out about a topic?

   First: _I decide to search for either an author, a title,_

   or a subject.

   Second: _____

   Third: _____

   Last: _____

3. You are looking for information to answer this research question:

   How did the United Farm Workers labor union help California farm workers?

   Write the key words you would enter into the computer.

   _____

4. You have heard that someone named Sorenson has written a book about César Chávez. Answer the questions.

   • What words would you enter to do a subject search for this book? _____

   • What kind of search would you do to find books written by this person?

   _____

   What word would you enter? _____

MORE ABOUT A COMPUTER CATALOG Find another book about farm workers. Write the title and author.

CONTENT AREA CONNECTIONS

Experiment with Music

DIRECTIONS Find out what scientists say about how music affects people. Research two or more articles. Take notes on a web.

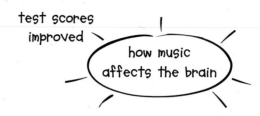

test scores improved

how music affects the brain

DIRECTIONS Design an experiment that uses the scientific process. Complete the chart.

Hypothesis Write your guess about what your experiment will prove.	_____ _____
Procedures: 1. What two similar groups of students will you use? What will each group do?	I will use two similar groups of _____ . Each group will _____ _____ .
2. What will be different about the two groups?	One group will _____ _____ . The other group will _____ _____ .
3. How will you check to see who learned the most?	I will see who learned the most by _____ _____ .
Results Which group learned more?	_____
Conclusion Was your hypothesis correct? State your conclusions.	_____

© Hampton-Brown

BUILD LANGUAGE AND VOCABULARY

The Ordinary as Art

Collection Walker Art Center, Minneapolis; Gift of Frederick R. Weisman in honor of his parents, William and May Weisman, 1988.

"I make my work out of my everyday experiences, which I find as perplexing and extraordinary as can be."
—Claes Oldenburg

> **Verb Tenses**
>
> A **present tense verb** says the action is happening now or happens all the time.
>   Art **inspires** people.
>
> A **past tense verb** shows that the action happened earlier, or in the past.
>   Primitive people **made** beautiful things.
>
> A **future tense verb** shows action that will happen later, or in the future.
>   Humans **will create** art in the future.

DIRECTIONS Use the correct tense of the verb in parentheses to complete each sentence. Write the verb tense you used.

1. Claes Oldenburg's family _____immigrated_____ to the U.S. from Sweden. (**immigrate**)   _____past tense_____

2. First, his family _____ in New York. (**settle**)   _____

3. In 1950, Oldenburg ___took___ classes at the Art Institute of Chicago. (**take**)   _____

4. Now he __is__ a well-known pop artist. (**be**)   _____

5. Future art fans _will loving_ his sculptures. (**love**)   _____

6. He often ___uses___ common objects like sandwiches and lipsticks as subject matter. (**use**)   _____

7. Sometimes, he ___makes___ his sculptures from recycled objects. (**make**)   _____

8. Many of his cloth sculptures ___ise___ very large. (**be**)   _____

9. In 1963, he ___made___ ice cream bars from fake fur, stuffing, and wood. (**make**)   _____

10. The ice cream bars ___it___ 19 inches long. (**be**)   _____

11. In 1988, he ___created___ a 51-foot-long spoon with a 1,200 pound cherry. (**create**)   _____

12. Imagine how high his new sculptures _____ in the future! (**reach**)   _____

© Hampton-Brown

Internet Words

New Words

animation

assemble

cyberspace

link

logo

official

operate

site

text

transfer

Relate Words

DIRECTIONS Work with a partner. Write the new words
where they belong.

You might <u>see</u> these things at an official Web site:	You can <u>do</u> these things in cyberspace:

Use Context Clues

DIRECTIONS Read the paragraph. Replace each
bold word with the correct new word.

I helped our computer teacher put together our school's _____official_____
1. approved

Web site. It took a long time to _____ all the information we
2. gather

wanted to include. We _____ a copy of our school
3. moved

_____ from another computer file and put the symbol on our
4. symbol

site. Then we typed some ____text____ that described our school.
5. words

We also added some ____line____ of our mascot, a roaring lion.
6. moving pictures

Finally, we added ___assemble___
7. connections

to other classes' pages. Now the page is

_____ 24 hours a day!
8. working

Home of
the Lions!

Links:
math classes
English classes
history classes

© Hampton-Brown

GRAMMAR: COUNT AND NONCOUNT NOUNS

A Class Home Page

DIRECTIONS Underline each noun in the passage. Then write each noun in the correct column.

    My <u>class</u> created a Web page about our dreams for the <u>future</u>. We wanted to share our goals with people everywhere.

    We encouraged good health. We explained the importance of vegetables in our diet. We provided information about the equipment we have in our gym.

    We have exciting ideas for adulthood. Some of us will use our energy to serve democracy. Others want to study science or play football. We want to make the world a better place. We hope visitors to our site will share our enthusiasm.

Count and Noncount Nouns

Count nouns have a singular and a plural form.
computer/computers
person/people

Noncount nouns have only one form for both singular and plural.
We have a lot of **software**.

Students share their dreams on a Web page.

Count Nouns	Noncount Nouns
1. _____class_____	14. _____future_____
2. _____people_____	15. _____share_____
3. _____	16. _____
4. _____	17. _____
5. _____	18. _____
6. _____	19. _____
7. _____	20. _____
8. _____	21. _____
9. _____	22. _____
10. _____	23. _____
11. _____	24. _____
12. _____	
13. _____	

Come With Me to Budapest

DIRECTIONS Anna created a home page. Write the correct articles to complete the text. Add articles only when you need to. See Handbook page 435 for examples of nouns that do not need articles.

Articles

Use **a** or **an** before a noun that is not specific.
   She clicks on **a link**.
   She finds **an image** of **a city**.

Use **the** before a specific noun.
   She likes **the image** of **Budapest** best.

Some nouns do not take articles before them.

Anna's Home Page

| File | Edit | Go | Favorites | Thu 9:32 AM |

Search

Back Forward Reload Home Stop Print

Budapest, on the Danube River, has many beautiful old buildings.

Hello. I am Anna. I am ___a___ student at
                          1.

Peterson Middle School. I am from Hungary. Hungary

is ___the___ country in ___the___ Europe. I
      2.   **3.**

still have relatives living in Budapest, which is

_____ capital of Hungary. They live in ___the___ apartment.
    4.   **5.**

Here's ___an___ interesting fact about ___The___ Budapest that I bet you
         6.   **7.**

don't know. The city is divided into two sections — Buda and Pest. Buda lies on ___the___
                                                                                    8.

west bank of the Danube River, and Pest lies on ___the___ east bank. My relatives live
                                                    9.

on the east side, but sometimes they take ___a___ walk or spend a day in Buda.
                                             10.

Just click on this link to see pictures of my relatives. You can also see ___a___
                                                                            11.

photograph I took of Budapest in ___the___ March last year.
                                    12.

© Hampton-Brown

Relate Steps in a Process

DIRECTIONS Write the steps Sarah followed to make her Web page.
Write each step as a command.

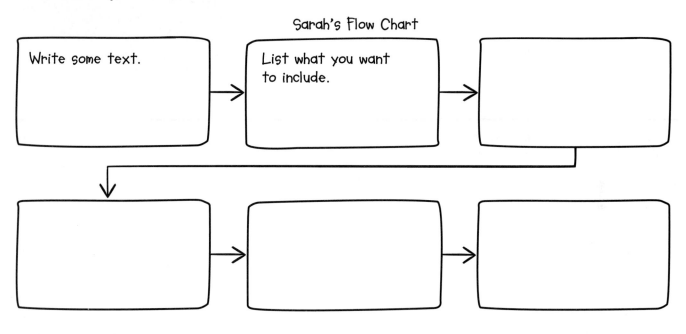

Sarah's Flow Chart

| Write some text. | List what you want to include. | |

DIRECTIONS What would your Web page be like? Use commands
to show the steps you would take to plan your page.

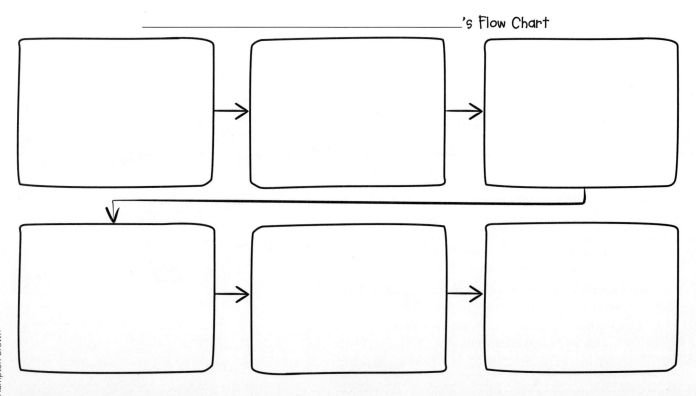

_____ 's Flow Chart

Nouns of the ℜoundtable

> **Nouns**
>
> A **common noun** names any person, place, thing, or idea. A **proper noun** names one particular person, place, thing, or idea.
>
> The **girl** likes **Artesia High School**.
>   common   proper
>
> A **concrete noun** names something you can see. An **abstract noun** names something you can't see.
>
> Sarah's **book** is full of creative **ideas**.
>   concrete   abstract

My common noun is "school."

"park"

"road"

Name a **common noun** for a place.

Name a **proper noun** for a person.

Name a **proper noun** for a thing.

Name a **common noun** for a thing.

Name a **concrete noun**.

Name a **proper noun** for a place.

Name an **abstract noun**.

Name a **common noun** for a person.

How to Play Nouns of the ℜoundtable

1. Form teams of three or four players.

2. Player 1 points to a space on the gameboard. The player gives an example of that kind of noun. Then each player on the team gives an example. Score 1 point for each correct answer. Group determines accuracy.

3. Player 2 points to a space and gives an example. The game continues until all the spaces have been chosen.

4. Total your score. Compare it to another team's score. The team with the most points wins.

CONTENT AREA CONNECTIONS

Evaluate a Home Page

DIRECTIONS What will your home page be like? Browse the Internet with a partner to get ideas. Complete the chart for each home page. Use what you like about them to help you plan your own!

Home Page Name: _____

Address: _____

Quality	None	Poor	Good	Great!
Is the home page appealing?				
Photos and graphics				
Use of color				
Use of sound				
Overall design				
Is the home page easy to use?				
Time it takes to appear				
Links to other sites				
Links to e-mail				
Readability of text				
Is the information of high quality?				
Accuracy				
Currentness of information				
Thoroughness				
Level of interest				

Summary: _____

_____

_____

_____

_____

Idioms

Locate and Use Definitions

DIRECTIONS Write what you think each idiom means. Check the meaning in the Glossary. If your meaning is correct, make a check. If it is not, write the correct meaning.

Idiom (phrase with a special meaning)	What I Think It Means	Confirmed / What It Means
Don't play dumb.	Don't act silly.	Don't act like you don't understand.
He knocked my head off.		
He was picking the brains of the computer.		
I checked it out.		
I had some time on my hands.		
I'll take care of her.		
It was a blur.		
They're history.		
What's the big idea?		
Your happiness is everything to me.		

MORE ABOUT IDIOMS Work with a partner. Role-play a conversation using idioms. Add other idioms you have heard. Ask other students to tell what the idioms mean.

Purposes of Dialogue

DIRECTIONS Read the story all the way through. Then look at the underlined dialogue. Write what the dialogue shows you about the characters or the action.

> **Dialogue**
>
> **Dialogue** is what characters say to each other. A writer uses dialogue to make a story interesting, show what the characters are like, and tell about some of the action.
>
> Most dialogue is set off by quotation marks.
>
> "We have lift off," Lieutenant Hiroko reported.

Story	Purpose of Dialogue
1. Lieutenant Hiroko burst into the room. "What is this mess?" she barked.	This shows that the lieutenant feels upset because of a mess. This tells what the story will be about.
2. "Blip, creek, blup," complained the little droid.	This shows that the little droid is trying to _____ _____ .
3. Hiroko flipped the switch on the droid's translator. "It's only spinach pasta and ketchup," said N411. Then, its feelings hurt, the droid added, "I was trying to fix you dinner."	The droid wanted _____ _____ . This shows _____ .
4. "Dinner? You were supposed to fix the land speeder, you little computer head," complained the lieutenant. "We're due out of here at 1800 hours!"	Now we know _____ . The lieutenant feels _____ because _____ .
5. "You've been very grouchy lately," said the droid as it swept pasta off the floor. "I think you should eat before we go."	The droid knows the lieutenant well enough _____ . It is trying to _____ .

MORE ABOUT DIALOGUE Write new dialogue for the characters in the picture. Have a partner tell what your dialogue shows about the characters or the action.

GRAMMAR: INDEFINITE ADJECTIVES

Friendly Uses

DIRECTIONS Answer each question.

1. Which indefinite adjectives may be used with either count or noncount nouns?

_____

2. Which indefinite adjective may be used in both positive and negative sentences?

_____

3. Which indefinite adjectives are used only with count nouns?

_____

Indefinite Adjectives

Use an **indefinite adjective** when you don't know the exact amount.

Use these before a count noun to tell **how many**:

many	a few	some
several	any	no

I have **many robots.**

Use these before a noncount noun to tell **how much**:

much	not much	a little
some	any	no

I need **a little help.**

In a negative sentence with noncount nouns, use **any** instead of **some**.

I didn't see **any robots.**

DIRECTIONS Complete each sentence. Use the correct indefinite adjective.

4. Robots help factory workers with _____many_____ tasks.
   much / many

5. These robots may get the job done, but they are _____ fun.
   not much / a few

6. In _____ years, robots may be much more advanced.
   a little / a few

7. Even today, there are _____ improvements in
   several / much

   robotic engineering.

8. In Japan, for example, _____ companies are
   much / some

   making robotic pets.

9. A computerized cat does not eat _____ food.
   several / any

10. An electronic dog only needs _____ programming.
    a little / a few

11. Of course, these pets don't give their owners _____ affection.
    any / some

12. In the future, there may be _____ limits to what robots can do!
    no / not much

Analyze Story Elements

DIRECTIONS Read the story. Complete the map.

A Daring Rescue

"The enemy won't get away with kidnapping Captain Tran," said Lupe to the rebel soldiers. "I'll get him back!"

She started the sand speeder and raced away from the rebel camp. The tall, orange dunes of the planet Borax stretched as far as she could see. Suddenly the sand speeder tilted sideways. Lupe climbed out and discovered a piece of dune shell sticking in one tire. She fixed the tire and continued on to the enemy camp.

Lupe hid her vehicle behind a dune. As soon as it was dark, she crept into camp. "Six tents," she murmured. "Which holds

Tran?" She used her life scanner and found him in the fourth tent. She was already dressed as an enemy guard so no one noticed her crawling into the tent.

"Here, put this enemy uniform on," she whispered to Tran. They hurried to start the sand speeder and raced over the dunes. They were free!

Tran and Lupe cruised into camp as the soldiers cheered.

"You saved my life, Lupe, and brought the rebels closer to victory," said Tran. "You are truly a brave soldier."

Map of Rising and Falling Action

Characters: _____   Setting: _____

Complication: _____

_____

_____

_____

Climax: _____

_____

_____

RISING ACTION

FALLING ACTION

Complication: _____

_____

_____

_____

Resolution: _____

_____

_____

Conflict: _____

GRAMMAR: ADJECTIVES

Be a Word Artist

DIRECTIONS Complete the story. Choose the precise adjective from each pair.

> **Adjectives**
>
> An **adjective** describes a noun or a pronoun.
>> An **unexpected** message flashes on the **fuzzy** screen. It looks **mysterious**.
>
> **Precise adjectives** paint a clear and vivid picture.
>> The **sleek**, **upgraded** computer has a **tricky** personality.

Blink, Flash, Blink . . .

Metin checked the green numbers on his _____*digital*_____ clock. It was
$\qquad$ **1. modern / digital**

midnight. He had been awake for _____ hours, thinking about math
$\qquad$ **2. two / some**

homework and the _____ report that was due for science class. He felt
$\qquad$ **3. big / monumental**

_____, but he couldn't sleep a wink. The _____
4. exhausted / tired $\qquad$ **5. strong / powerful**

storm that was rattling the windows and flinging raindrops down on the roof didn't help either.

Metin snuggled down, pulled his _____ quilt up around his chin, and
$\qquad$ **6. warm / toasty**

stared at Conrad, his computer.

Conrad stared back. Then . . . blink, flash, blink. Words flickered on the

_____ screen: "Get some _____ sleep, Metin.
7. colored / blue-green $\qquad$ **8. refreshing / good**

You've got that science report, baseball practice. . ."

When Metin woke up, the sun was sparkling on the grass. It was a

_____ day. Jumping out of bed, he remembered the
9. glorious / nice

_____ message. "What a weird dream!" he said.
10. bizarre / different

WRITING: A FRIENDLY LETTER

Lines from Louis

DIRECTIONS Pretend you are Louis, the computer. Write a friendly letter to Kevin.

Friendly Letter
A **friendly letter** is written to someone you know. In a friendly letter you can share your feelings and tell what is going on in your life.

In the **heading**, write your address and today's date.

_____
_____
_____

In the **greeting**, write the word *Dear* and the name of your friend.

_____ ,

In the **body** of the letter, ask Kevin about his day and describe your day. Include details that tell about some things that could really happen and some that are science fiction.

Write a **closing** like *Sincerely, Love, Yours truly, Always,* or *Your friend.* Then write your **signature.**

_____ ,
_____

MORE ABOUT FRIENDLY LETTERS Give your letter to a partner. Have your partner write back.

© Hampton-Brown

UNIT 2 MIND MAP

Discoveries

DIRECTIONS Use the mind map to write about making discoveries. As you read the selections in this unit, add new ideas you learn about discoveries.

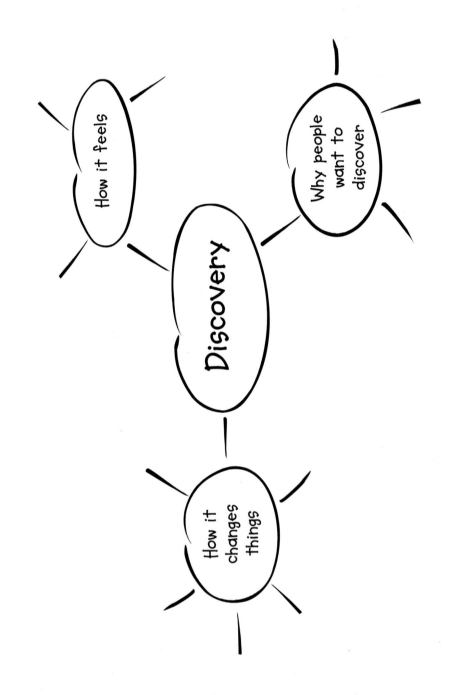

Two Ways to Go

DIRECTIONS Choose a coordinating conjunction to join each pair of sentences. Write the compound sentence.

Coordinating Conjunctions					
and	but	for	or	so	yet

Compound Sentences

A **compound sentence** is made up of two independent clauses. A **coordinating conjunction** joins the two clauses.

Kumar loves to hike, **but** Ashna loves to rock climb.

1. Get ready to hike the Grand Canyon. It's a grand adventure!

   Get ready to hike the Grand Canyon, for it's a grand adventure!

   _____

2. You need to take plenty of water and snacks. You might get sick.

   _____

   _____

3. Rangers recommend four liters of water for an all-day hike. Hikers need trail bars or other healthy snacks.

   _____

   _____

4. From the South Rim, you can hike down Bright Angel Trail. From the South Rim, you can take the South Kaibab Trail.

   _____

   _____

5. Drinking water is available along the Bright Angel Trail. There's no water on the South Kaibab.

   _____

   _____

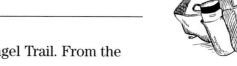

6. Either way, hiking in the Grand Canyon is difficult. You need to be prepared.

   _____

   _____

Words to Explore

New Words

barrier

difficulty

discover

expedition

explore

fur trade

journey

territory

the unknown

wilderness

Relate Words

DIRECTIONS Use the new words to complete the word map.

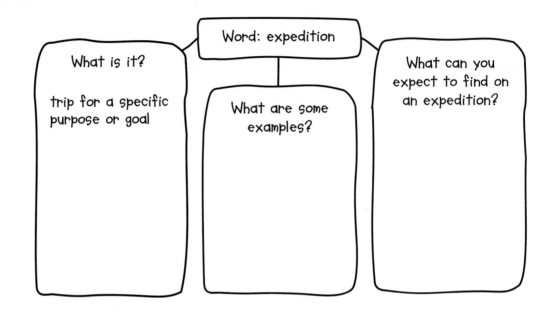

Use New Words in Context

DIRECTIONS Use your word map to write a paragraph that tells what an expedition is.

_____

_____

_____

_____

_____

_____

_____

_____

_____

GRAMMAR: PHRASES AND CLAUSES

Around the Rapids

Steep mountain passes and roaring river rapids made it impossible for Lewis and Clark to find a water route to the Pacific.

Phrases and Clauses

A **phrase** is a group of related words that does not have a subject and a predicate.

during the day

A **clause** is a group of words that has a subject and a predicate. An **independent clause** can stand alone as a sentence.

while **they traveled**

They drew new maps.

DIRECTIONS Write *P* for a phrase and *C* for a clause. Use the phrase and the clause to write a simple sentence.

1. ___P___ with a team of soldiers, rivermen, and volunteers

   ___C___ Lewis and Clark started up the Missouri River

   Lewis and Clark started up the Missouri River with a team

   of soldiers, rivermen, and volunteers.

2. _____ they had the job of finding a water route to the Pacific Ocean

   _____ as members of the Corps of Discovery

   _____

   _____

   _____

3. _____ York helped the Corps build good relations with many Native Americans

   _____ an important member of the team

   _____

   _____

   _____

DIRECTIONS Read the compound sentence. Identify the two independent clauses. Write each clause as a simple sentence.

4. The Corps struggled over the pass, and they descended into Travelers' Rest in Flathead Valley.

   _____

   _____

Expedition Goals and Outcomes

DIRECTIONS Read the article about two 21st century explorers.

The Bancroft Arnesen Expedition

In November of 2000, Ann Bancroft and Liv Arnesen set out to cross the continent of Antarctica on skis. They knew that an expedition across a frozen landmass bigger than the United States would not be easy. The explorers did it to show that people can make dreams of adventure come true.

On their way, Liv and Ann crossed huge crevasses, cracks in the ice that could be hundreds of feet deep and wide enough to swallow a person. To climb mountains, they attached crampons to their boots. These spikes bit into the ice for better traction.

The biggest challenge for the expedition, however, was the lack of wind. Without wind to fill their sails, the women had to pull their 250-pound supply sleds with arm- and leg-power alone.

Sore feet, injured wrists, and headaches from the cold and altitude did not stop Liv and Ann. In February of 2001, just before the start of the brutal Antarctic winter, they became the first women in history to cross Antarctica on foot and skis.

Bancroft and Arnesen pull sleds across Antarctica.

DIRECTIONS Use information from the article to complete the chart.

Expedition Goal	Obstacles	Outcome
	crevasses	

Summary:

Lewis's Scrapbook

DIRECTIONS Write a second sentence to complete each caption in Lewis's scrapbook. Use a pronoun in each sentence. Circle the pronoun. Be sure that the pronoun agrees with the antecedent.

I was President Jefferson's secretary.

Jefferson chose (me) to lead the expedition.

_____

York helped in many ways.

_____

_____

William Clark was my valuable co-leader.

_____

_____

The Corps built Fort Clatsop.

_____

_____

Sacagawea helped out.

_____

We have seen grizzly bears.

_____

WRITING: A JOURNAL ENTRY

Dear Journal

DIRECTIONS Imagine you are William Clark. Write journal entries to tell about your expedition. Include facts and opinions. Discuss the entries with your group.

> **A Journal**
>
> A **journal** tells about someone's personal thoughts and feelings. A journal entry can contain both **facts** and **opinions**.
>
> • A **fact** is a statement you can prove.
>
> • An **opinion** is a statement that tells what you think or feel about something.

Entry 1: Tell how you prepared for the trip.

Date: _____

Today I gathered _____

I feel _____

Entry 2: Tell about the environment on one part of the trip.

Date: _____

The weather today was _____

We saw _____

along the way and _____

Entry 3: Tell what you discovered.

Date: _____

One thing I discovered today was _____

The discovery makes me feel _____

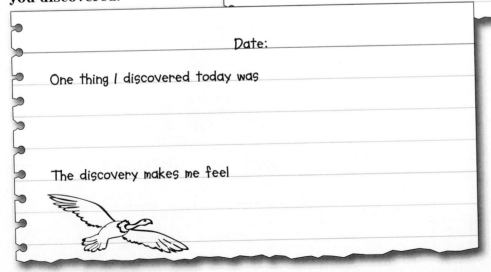

© Hampton-Brown

RESEARCH SKILLS

Use an Encyclopedia Index

DIRECTIONS Study the entries from an encyclopedia index. Then answer the questions.

Encyclopedia Index
Each set of encyclopedias has a volume called an **Index**. The index gives the volume and page numbers for all the entries about a topic in the entire encyclopedia.

volume and page number
This means the article is in the P volume and starts on page 730.

index heading
This is a main topic. It is also the title of an article.

index entry
This is the title of an article related to the main topic.

Prairie [geography] **P: 730** *with picture and map*
    Conservation (To maintain the quality of life)
        Ci: 976
    Flower (Flowers of prairies and dry plains)
        F: 286 *with pictures*
    Grassland **G: 329** *with picture*
    Plant (Grasslands) **P: 525**; *picture on* **P: 527**
Prairie chicken [bird] **P: 731**
    Bird (Birds of grasslands) **B: 336** *with picture*
Prairie dog [animal] **P: 732** *with pictures*
    Animal *picture on* **A: 477**

subheading
When an article has special sections, a subheading might appear.

1. In which volume would you find the article "Prairie chicken"? ____P____

2. Where would you look to see a map of a prairie? Write the article title, volume, and page number. _____

3. The article "Flower" has a section about flowers of the prairies and dry plains. What other information might that article contain? _____

   _____

4. "Grassland" is one of four articles that are related to the same main topic. What is that main topic? _____

   Name another article related to that topic. _____

5. In the article "Bird," what subheading would you look under to learn about other birds of the prairie? _____

6. Which articles have pictures of prairie dogs?

   _____   _____

CONTENT AREA CONNECTIONS

Rates of Travel

DIRECTIONS Figure out rates of travel in the 1800s and today.

1 Study the formula.

$$\frac{\text{distance}}{\text{time}} \quad \frac{\text{X miles}}{\text{X days}} = \quad \begin{array}{c}\text{X} \\ \text{average} \\ \text{rate}\end{array} \quad \text{miles/day}$$

2 Use the data and formula to find out the average rate
Lewis and Clark traveled on their whole trip.

With a calculator:

1. Enter the number *8000*.
2. Press the ÷ key.
3. Enter the number *862*.
4. Press the = key.
5. Write your answer.

_____

By hand:

$$\frac{8000 \text{ miles}}{862 \text{ days}} = \underline{\hspace{2cm}} \text{ miles/day}$$

3 Now calculate the average rate of travel by foot and by train for each part
of the Lewis and Clark journey. Use the formula. Write your answers.

Destinations	Distance (miles)	Time (days)		Average Rate (miles per day)	
		By Foot	By Train	By Foot	By Train
Wood River to Fort Mandan	about 1,510	164	1		
Wood River to Fort Clatsop	about 3,700	551	2		

4 Compare the average rates of travel. Discuss your thoughts with a partner.
- A train can go for 24 hours per day. How does that affect the average rate of travel?
- What can you say about travel in the 1800s and travel today?

© Hampton-Brown

Space Exploration Words

New Words

- astronaut
- gravity
- launch
- Manned Maneuvering Unit
- orbit
- routine monitoring and maintenance
- satellite
- scientific testing and experimentation
- smoke-detection system
- space laboratory
- spacecraft
- tether
- weightlessness

Relate Words and Locate Definitions

DIRECTIONS Complete the chart with your group. Then use the Glossary to check the meaning of each new word. Do you need to make any changes in your chart?

Sometimes astronauts float above the Earth.

Categories	New Words
Technology	spacecraft
Traveling in Space	gravity
Living in Space	astronaut
Working in Space	space laboratory

Use New Words in Context

DIRECTIONS Use the new words to tell what you know about space exploration.

_____

_____

_____

_____

GRAMMAR: ACTIVE AND PASSIVE VERBS

Animals in Space

Active and Passive Verbs

A verb is **active** if the subject performs the action.

In the 1950s, **scientists sent** dogs into space.

A verb is **passive** if the subject does not perform the action.

In the 1960's, several **chimps were sent** into space.

TOUCH DOWN!		
On July 20, 1969, Neil Armstrong walked on the moon!	**LAUNCH! FREE SPACE ➡** Many animals were sent into space in the 20th century. Passive. Scientists sent many animals into space in the 20th century.	Dogs and monkeys were sent into space.
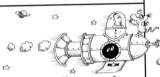 Eventually, people were sent into space.	**How to Play:** *Animals in Space* 1. Play in a small group. One person is the "space official." The others are the players. 2. Each player chooses a small object as a game piece and places it on LAUNCH. Players use a coin to move.  = 1 space  = 2 spaces	In 1948, a rhesus monkey named Albert rode in a rocket.
Chimps were taught to perform many human tasks.	3. In turn, each player reads aloud the sentence and identifies the verb as **active** or **passive**. If the verb is passive, player changes the verb to active and says the new sentence aloud. 4. The "space official" judges accuracy.	Scientists sent many dogs into space.
Chimpanzees were also chosen for space travel in the early days.	5. **Stay** on the space if your answer is correct. **Go back** one space for each incorrect response. 6. The first player to reach TOUCH DOWN! wins.	In 1957, a husky named Laika traveled in a satellite called Sputnik 2.
Laika was nicknamed "Muttnik" by the American press.	**FREE SPACE!** Two dogs named Strelka and Belka orbited Earth 18 times. *Active.* *The subject (dogs) performs the action.* **STAY ON FREE SPACE**	Laika was sent into space by the Soviets.

© Hampton-Brown

To the Outer Galaxy!

DIRECTIONS Add a prepositional phrase to each sentence. Use prepositions from the chart or others. See Handbook page 456 for more prepositions.

Prepositional Phrases

A **prepositional phrase** starts with a **preposition** and ends with a noun or pronoun. Prepositional phrases add details to sentences.

The astronaut floats **outside the spacecraft**.

Some Prepositions

Location	Time	Direction	Others
under outside in	before during until	through into toward	from at for

1. Astronauts make careful preparations _before a space mission_____ .

2. They may be on board _____ .

3. Fresh oxygen is circulated _____ .

4. Meals are eaten _____ .

5. Astronauts need to work _____ .

6. Commercial enterprises send experiments to be done _____ .

7. Astronauts may help us find cures _____ .

8. Outside the capsule, astronauts must be tethered _____ .

9. Astronauts may stay on board _____ .

10. In the future, some people may spend their lives wandering _____ .

11. Would you like to live in a space station _____ ?

12. Will your family travel _____ ?

MORE ABOUT PREPOSITIONAL PHRASES Write a paragraph about where you want to live in the future. Use at least one prepositional phrase in each sentence.

Construction of the International Space Station began in orbit in 1998. When it is complete in 2005, it will have room for seven astronauts and scientists.

How Accurate Is It?

DIRECTIONS Read the student essays. Then compare them with "Space Exploration" to evaluate their accuracy.

Evaluate Literature

When you **evaluate nonfiction**, consider how accurate the information is. One way to evaluate accuracy is to compare the selection with other writing on the subject.

Chang's Essay

People have always been curious about space and wondered how to explore it. Several hundred years ago rockets were developed.

In the last half of the 20th century, machines made by humans have traveled to the moon and beyond. First, animals were sent into space to see if it would be safe for humans.

Several hundred people and many more animals, plants, and insects have traveled in space. More than two dozen astronauts have orbited the Earth many times.

At the beginning of the 21st century, a space station was built through cooperation among many nations. Some day there might even be hotels in space!

Laura's Essay

The idea of traveling in space has always appealed to people. Hundreds of our brightest minds have worked to solve the problems of space travel.

In 1957 Jules Verne wrote a story about traveling in space. His ideas became reality when the first human being walked on the moon in 1961.

Since then, more than 3000 people and millions of other living beings have traveled in space. People have even lived in space for many days at a time.

People who travel in space are called astronauts and are considered great explorers. Lots of people want to go, but only a few are chosen. You have to be young and good-looking to travel in space.

1. Are the facts in the essays correct? Underline statements in each that do not agree with the facts in "Space Exploration."

2. Which essay is more accurate? Write your conclusion.

_____ 's essay is more accurate because _____

_____

_____

_____.

MORE ABOUT EVALUATING ACCURACY Another way to evaluate accuracy is to find proof of the facts. Work with a partner. Brainstorm ways to check the facts in the student essays. Check the facts and report your findings to your class.

SUM IT UP

Relate Main Ideas and Details

DIRECTIONS Use your notes for "Space Exploration" to add details to the tree diagram. Tell more about each main idea.

Details:

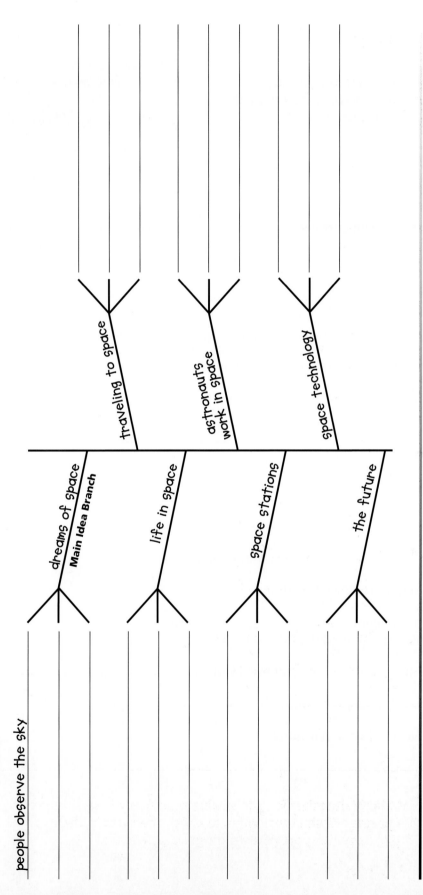

Main Idea Branch: dreams of space — traveling to space

life in space — astronauts work in space

space stations — space technology

the future

people observe the sky

DIRECTIONS Use one main idea and the details to write a paragraph.

GRAMMAR: VERBS

An Inspiration

DIRECTIONS Choose a verb from the box to complete each sentence. Some verbs may be used more than once. Tell what kind of verb you used.

is	have	seem	encourage
are	has	visit	travel
can	said	work	explore

Verbs

An **action verb** tells what the subject does.
Many people **enjoy** science fiction programs.

A **linking verb** connects, or links, the subject of a sentence to a word in the predicate.
Science fiction **is** fascinating.
Some events **seem** possible.

When a **helping verb** is needed, it comes before the action verb.
The future **may** surprise us.

Kind of Verb

1. Science fiction movies and TV programs _____have_____ entertained people for decades. _____helping_____

2. They _____ helped to break down prejudices, too. _____

3. On some TV programs, crew members from many countries

   _____ together for the common good. _____

4. In movies and on TV, characters from distant planets

   _____ the galaxy with human crew members. _____

5. They _____ the universe. _____

6. The males and females _____ equally capable. _____

7. The crew members are respectful of one another, and they

   _____ content to work together. _____

8. Occasionally, the crew members _____ distant planets for business or a vacation. _____

9. Good science fiction _____ an inspiration. _____

10. It makes it seem possible that the entire universe

    _____ learn to live in harmony. _____

WRITING: A PERSONAL NARRATIVE

Out of This World

DIRECTIONS Write about an imaginary trip to the first space hotel. Make a list of things you could do or see. Then choose one or two to write about.

Personal Narrative
A story that tells about something that happened to you is a **personal narrative**. A personal narrative is written in the first person.

Title: _____

In the **beginning**, tell when and where you went on your trip.

In _____ I went to _____ .

First, I _____

Use first-person pronouns. Use **order words** to tell when something happened.

_____

_____ .

Then, I _____

_____

In the **middle**, tell more about the trip. Describe what you saw and did. Tell how you felt about your experiences.

_____ .

After that, I _____

_____

_____

_____ .

I felt _____

_____

_____ .

At the **end**, tell what you will remember the most.

I will always remember _____

_____

_____

RESEARCH SKILLS

Readers' Guide

DIRECTIONS Study the entries from the *Readers' Guide*.
Then answer the questions.

Readers' Guide

The *Readers' Guide to Periodical Literature* is an index of articles from periodicals, or magazines. The articles are organized by subject. The guide is updated each year.

subject heading — **SPACE FLIGHT TO MARS**
See also

related subjects in the *Readers' Guide* —
Mars Climate Orbiter
Mars Global Surveyor
Mars Polar Lander
Mars Society
Mars vehicles

Faster, cheaper, dumber [Mars Polar Lander accident and other problems for NASA's Mars exploration] C. W. Petit. il *U.S. News & World Report* v128 no14 p25 Ap 10 2000 — illustrations

Mars probes: did 'cheaper' and 'faster' preclude 'better'? W. B. Scott. *Aviation Week & Space Technology* v151 no25 p11+ D 20–27 1999 — volume number

Mars reassessment to Goldin in March. M. A. Dornheim. *Aviation Week & Space Technology* v151 no25 p129 D 20–27 1999 — issue number

article title — NASA ponders new path to Mars. J. R. Asker and others. *Aviation Week & Space Technology* v151 no24 p35 D 13 1999 — page number

Reports will urge overhaul and delays to NASA's Mars missions. A. Lawler. il tab *Science* v287 no5459 p1722-3 Mr 10 2000

Reviewers see red over recent Mars programs. R. Cowen. il *Science News* v157 no14 p215 Ap 1 2000 — month and year of magazine

title of periodical (magazine) —
Special report: sending astronauts to Mars. il *Scientific American* v282 no3 p40–63 Mr 2000

1. What is the main subject of these entries? **SPACE FLIGHT TO MARS** _____

2. Which of these subjects is <u>not</u> related to the main subject: Mars Society, Jupiter's

   Moons, or Mars vehicles? _____

3. Which article is the most recent? _____

4. "Special Report: Sending Astronauts to Mars" is an article in *Scientific American*.

   On which page does it begin? _____

5. Which periodical contains the article "NASA Ponders New Path to Mars"?

   _____

6. In which volume and issue of *Science News* can you find the article "Reviewers See

   Red over Recent Mars Programs"? _____

Interpret Symbols

DIRECTIONS Read the poem. Think about the symbols the poet uses. Then complete the chart.

Symbols

A **symbol** is something that stands for a feeling, mood, or idea. Poets use **symbolism** to give their writing deeper meaning.

Many Times Blessed
— **Phyllis Edwards**

Eagle parent,	Monkey friend,	Moon partner,
Owl guide,	Fox companion,	Night cradle.

Symbol	What the Symbol Is Like	What the Poet Wants to Communicate
eagle owl	strong, brave _____	The poet has strong, brave parents and _____ guides.
monkey fox	_____ _____	The poet's friends are both _____ _____ .
moon night	_____ _____	The poet feels _____ _____ at night.
The poet feels blessed with _____ _____ .		

DIRECTIONS Write a short poem that uses symbols. Read your poem to a partner. Ask your partner to identify each symbol and what it stands for.

_____

_____

_____

_____

BUILD LANGUAGE AND VOCABULARY

My Own Story

Complex Sentences

A **complex sentence** has one independent clause and one or more dependent clauses. An independent clause can stand alone as a sentence.

When I was fourteen,
dependent clause

my family moved to the United States.
independent clause

In many complex sentences, a **subordinating conjunction** signals the beginning of the dependent clause.

although	if	since	where	until
because	as	when	while	so

DIRECTIONS Read each sentence. Underline the independent clause. Circle the dependent clause. Then write the subordinating conjunction.

1. We left Haiti behind (when my family came to the United States.) _____when_____

2. At first, we were lonely because we missed our friends. _____

3. Since we are a large family, we had each other for support. _____

4. We looked all over for an apartment where we could live. _____

5. Until we found an apartment, we stayed with our cousins. _____

6. While Papa and Mama looked for work, I took care of my brothers. _____

7. I was unhappy because I had no time to meet kids my own age. _____

8. I would not let my brothers watch TV until they had played outside. _____

9. I met my best friend, Dominique, as I was helping André ride a bike. _____

10. Dominique wanted to get to know me when she saw me helping my brother. _____

11. Although it took a while, the boys developed friendships, too. _____

12. If you are good-hearted, people will want to be your friend. _____

Beauty Pageant Words

New Words

acute

anxiously

beauty

clue

contestant

defy

feature

inspire

pageant

Paraphrase Definitions

DIRECTIONS Finish the sentences about the new words.

1. If you are a contestant, you are _____ in a contest _____ .

2. A pageant is a kind of _____ .

3. If you defy a rule, you _____ it.

4. Something or someone who has beauty has _____ .

5. If you wait anxiously for news, you wait in a _____ way.

6. You inspire people when you _____ .

7. A feature is a part of your _____ .

8. A clue is a _____ .

9. If something is acute, it is _____ .

Use New Words in Context

DIRECTIONS Read the paragraph. Add the missing words.

Last night, I watched a beauty _____ pageant _____ on TV. Each state had
                                        10.

one _____ , and every girl was a real _____
            11.   12.

to look at. We looked for _____ to predict the winner. All the
                                    13.

contestants looked their best, and every _____ of every face
                                                    14.

was pretty. One contestant _____ the judges and had to leave
                                    15.

the stage. Another contestant sang a beautiful song and _____
                                                                    16.

me to take singing lessons again. All the contestants had _____
                                                                    17.

feelings of worry as they waited _____ to see who would win.
                                            18.

The Island of Hispaniola

The Dominican Republic takes up the eastern two-thirds of the island of Hispaniola.

Complex Sentences

A **complex sentence** has one independent clause and one or more dependent clauses. An independent clause can stand alone as a sentence. A **subordinating conjunction** signals the beginning of the dependent clause.

Before the Spanish settled Hispaniola,
dependent clause

Arawak farmers had lived there for centuries.
independent clause

DIRECTIONS Use a subordinating conjunction to combine each pair of sentences into a complex sentence.

Some Subordinating Conjunctions	
when	while
until	after
because	if
before	since
although	as

1. The Dominican Republic is a country. It shares the island of Hispaniola with its neighbor, Haiti.

   Although the Dominican Republic is a country, it shares

   the island of Hispaniola with its neighbor, Haiti.

2. The island of Hispaniola is fertile. It has always been a good place for farming.

   _____

   _____

3. Sugar is very important to the island's economy. Rice, cotton, and coffee are grown on the farms, too.

   _____

   _____

4. The economy of Hispaniola is primarily agricultural. The island has rich deposits of nickel, gold, and silver.

   _____

   _____

5. Travel to this Caribbean island. You will find a huge variety of plants and animals.

   _____

   _____

Whose View?

DIRECTIONS Read each passage. Write the point of view and explain how you identified it.

Narrator's Point of View

The **first-person point of view** uses first-person pronouns to tell about the narrator's own life and feelings.

 I felt proud of **our** performance in the play.

The **third-person point of view** uses third-person pronouns to tell about someone else's life and feelings.

 She thought **her** computer was talking to **her**.

From "The Lion King Goes to Broadway"

> Taymor accepted the challenge, putting all her years of theatrical experience into creating a new concept for *The Lion King*. When she began to address the question of how to bring the animal characters to life, she knew she did not want to hide the actors inside big animal suits.

Point of View: _____

Clues: It has _____ .

It tells about _____

_____ .

From "Inspiration"

> At those times I get real quiet and let the thoughts, melodies, or rhythms just roll around in my head until one surfaces that I can work with. I call these "fishing expeditions." . . . I've learned to pay attention to what is going on around me.

Point of View: _____

Clues: It has _____ .

It tells about _____

_____ .

From "User Friendly"

> As I walked by my computer table, I pressed my computer Louis's on button. The computer's screen glowed greenly, displaying the message: Good Morning, Kevin.
> I had almost walked by Louis, when I noticed there was another message on the screen.

Point of View: _____

Clues: It has _____ .

It tells about _____

_____ .

From "Space Exploration"

> On board were the seven astronauts who had arrived on *Atlantis*, and three other astronauts who were already in Mir. They returned to Earth with the results of the experiments they had done while in space.

Point of View: _____

Clues: It has _____ .

It tells about _____

SUM IT UP

Summarizing a Teen Success

DIRECTIONS Follow the steps to summarize a selection.

1 Read the news story.

Angie Ignacio

Teen Center a Success

Section 1: Introducing Angie

"What inspires you to volunteer at the Teen Center?" I asked Angie Ignacio. "I want to help other kids the way people have helped me."

Angie is a good example of how immigrants are improving life for everyone in our community. Angie spends her Thursday evenings at the Teen Center, sponsored by the Filipino Community Coalition.

Section 2: Benefits of the Center

Teens flock to the Center every week night to play basketball, study with friends, and listen to CDs. Adults and trained peer-advisors like Angie are always available.

Neighbors feel that the Center has improved the environment of the area. "There aren't so many kids standing on the street corners," stated a local merchant. "The kids who come from the Center are polite and don't cause trouble in my shop."

2 Cross out the details that are unimportant. Then write a summary statement for each section.

Section 1: Introducing Angie	Section 2: Benefits of the Center
Details: Angie volunteers at Teen Center ~~wants to help others~~ Thursday evenings immigrants are improving life run by the Filipino CC	Details: teens go every night basketball, study, CDs adults and peer-advisors not so many kids on the corners neighbors feel it improves the area
Summary Statement:	Summary Statement:

3 Use the summary statements to write a summary paragraph for the entire selection. Combine related sentences with subordinating conjunctions.

_____

_____

_____

© Hampton-Brown

As Simple as a Simile

DIRECTIONS Look at the object in each picture. Write similes that compare the object to other objects. Get ideas from the word box.

Simile

A **simile** makes a comparison using words such as *like* or *as*.

Her hair sparkled **like diamonds**.

Objects for Comparison		
a food	a piece of equipment	an animal
something in nature	a musical instrument	a plant or tree
something fast	a sporting tool (ball, bat, net)	something slow
something round	something frightening	something huge
something messy	a character in a story	something loud

1. The old jacket smelled _____.

2. _____

3. The library computer sounds _____.

4. _____

DIRECTIONS Write a description of the picture. Include similes for the shapes, sounds, smells, sizes, or textures you might find in the scene.

_____

_____

_____

_____

_____

_____

Analyze Propaganda

DIRECTIONS Follow the steps to analyze propaganda.

1 Write the name of the propaganda technique used in each example.

1. New! Smoother Glide! Longer Lasting Ink! Buy *Write Right* pens today.

_____

2. Be part of the *Right* group. Join the thousands of top students who use *Write Right* pens.

_____

3. Look at these smears from ordinary pens. What a mess! Use *Write Right* pens for neat work.

_____

4. "I use *Write Right* pens to write my best-selling books," says Carolina Montez, author of *From Rio to New York* and *A Walk Along the Beach*.

_____

Propaganda Techniques

Advertisers use **propaganda** to convince others to believe or do something. Propaganda uses several **techniques**.

- A **glittering generality** uses words like *Better! New!*
- A **testimonial** uses well-known people to convince you.
- The **bandwagon** technique tells you to do something because other people are doing it.
- **Name-calling** is saying bad things about another product.

2 Think about four ads you saw this week. Complete the chart.

Product Being Advertised	Propaganda Technique Used	Why One Ad was Most Convincing
		The _____ ad is most convincing because _____ _____ _____ .

3 Choose a product. Draw and write two ads for the product. Use two different propaganda techniques. Share your ads with a partner. Discuss which is more effective and why.

5. Here I used the _____

_____

propaganda technique.

6. I showed this technique by _____

_____

_____

_____

_____ .

7. Here I used the _____

_____

propaganda technique.

8. I showed this technique by _____

_____

_____

_____

_____ .

MORE ABOUT PROPAGANDA What other ads have you seen or heard? Clip newspaper or magazine ads or tape radio or television ads and discuss them with a partner. Identify the technique used in each ad. Select the two most effective ads to share with the class.

An Immigrant's Contribution

DIRECTIONS Research and prepare a report about a famous immigrant's contributions. Follow these steps.

1 Plan Your Research Write answers to the questions.

- Which immigrant will I research? _____

_____

- What key words might help me find good Web sites or information in a

library catalog? _____

- What resources will I use? _____

_____

Sound recordings and videos can make your report more interesting.

2 Look Up Information Take notes. You might want to use a K-W-L chart.

3 Prepare a Multimedia Report Organize your notes and write your report. Answer the questions to help you decide what music, recordings, photos or other visuals will make your report even better!

- What is the most interesting thing I discovered about the immigrant's contributions?

How will I highlight this in my report? _____

_____

_____

- What sound recording will go with my report? Explain how it will be helpful.
  ☐ TV or radio clip   ☐ Web site download   ☐ CD or tape

_____

_____

- What visuals will I use?
  ☐ charts, diagrams   ☐ drawings   ☐ photos   ☐ video

4 Make a Presentation Arrange a time to present your report to the class. Allow time to set up any equipment you'll need for sharing the sound recordings or visuals.

Meaningful Words

New Words

free 1. *adj.*
not being under
someone
else's control
2. *adj./adv.*
without cost

land 1. *n.* part of
the earth's surface
that is not
covered by water,
the ground 2. *v.*
bring or come to
the shore 3. *v.*
come down or
bring to rest on a
surface

roots 1. *n.* plant
parts that grow
under the ground
2. *n.* beginnings of
a family, ancestry
3. *v.* cheers for
people in a
contest

Use Multiple Meanings

DIRECTIONS Read each sentence. Write the one new
word that fits in both blanks.

1. Every year many people leave family ____roots____ behind among the

   ____roots____ of ancient forests.

2. They _____ in the United States, a _____ of freedom.

3. Some boats and planes provide _____ transportation for

   passengers moving to this _____ country.

4. A fisherman tries to _____ a fish at the pier and watches a plane

   full of immigrants _____ at the airport across the highway.

5. The fisherman thinks about his family back in Sri Lanka and silently

   _____ for all the hopeful people who come to grow new

   _____ in this country.

Use Context Clues

DIRECTIONS Read the passage. Write the meaning of each
underlined word that fits in the sentence.

   Last summer I discovered a lot about my <u>roots</u> and my
family's history. Some of my ancestors were slaves. Others were
<u>free</u> farmers who grew crops on the <u>land</u> between the North and
the South. Although their lives were different, they all believed in
doing what was best for their families.

6. roots _____

   _____

7. free _____

   _____

8. land _____

© Hampton-Brown

Conclusions About Messages

DIRECTIONS Think about the message in each poem.
Then complete the chart.

Poem Title	Cultural Backgrounds in the Poem	The Message
"Saying Yes"	Chinese American	Be equally proud of all your cultural backgrounds.
"Still Finding Out"		
"Roots"		

DIRECTIONS Read the poem. Add information about it to the chart.
Tell a partner which of the four poems you like best and why.

Earth Child
— P. R. E.

They say I have no homeland;
I left my place of birth.

They say I lack identity;
I hail both East and West.

They say I have no roots;
I've lived both there and here.

The world is my homeland,

My identity the globe.

My soul is deep-rooted
in all of Mother Earth.

MORE ABOUT POETRY Find another poem you like and read it to the class.
Ask your classmates to tell you what message they hear in the poem.

Name _____   Date _____

Using Maps and Globes

DIRECTIONS Label each type of map. What do maps of that type show? List the main features.

Types of Maps		
physical	historical	road
political	product	globe

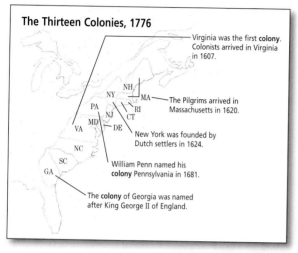

1. _____

_____

_____

2. _____

_____

_____

3. _____

_____

_____

DIRECTIONS Complete the sentences.

4. A _____ is a model of the Earth.

5. A _____ map shows the streets and highways of an area.

6. A _____ map shows goods that are produced in an area.

Conflict and Resolution

DIRECTIONS Use the mind map to show your ideas about conflicts and resolutions. As you read the selections in this unit, add new ideas you learn about conflicts and ways to resolve them.

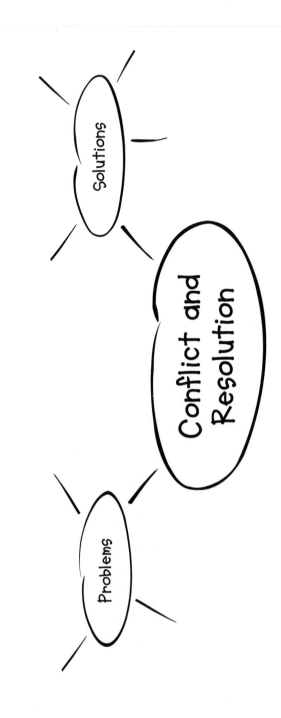

Who? What? When?

DIRECTIONS Underline the relative clause in each sentence. Circle the relative pronoun.

1. The Liberty Bell is a symbol (that) many Americans have seen.

2. It is a special bell that Americans respect.

3. The Pennsylvania Assembly ordered the bell to honor the work of William Penn whom the assemblymen admired.

4. The famous bell, which was made in London in 1751, rang out on July 8, 1776.

5. Citizens who heard it ring had come to listen to the first public reading of the Declaration of Independence.

6. Soon after, something happened that made the bell crack.

7. Two craftsmen, whose names were John Pass and John Stow, made a new bell from the original bell.

8. The Liberty Bell, which is now silent, still sends a powerful message.

> **Relative Clauses**
>
> A **relative clause** is one kind of dependent clause used in a complex sentence. It tells more about a person or thing.
>
> > The Liberty Bell, **which is in Philadelphia,** symbolizes freedom.
> >
> > A group **who wanted to outlaw slavery** gave the bell its name.
>
> A relative clause begins with a **relative pronoun**. Use **who, whom,** or **whose** for people. Use **which** for things. Use **that** for people or things.

"Proclaim liberty throughout all the land unto all the inhabitants thereof."
—Liberty Bell Inscription

DIRECTIONS Write complex sentences that contain relative clauses.

9. A teacher whom I like took us to see the Liberty Bell. _____

_____

10. _____

_____

11. _____

_____

12. _____

_____

Name _____ Date _____

Constitutional Words

Locate and Use Definitions

DIRECTIONS Use the Glossary to make a personal vocabulary card for each new word. On a separate sheet of paper, draw a picture to go with each word.

Amendments

Word: Bill of Rights Definition: first ten amendments to the Constitution Sentence: The Bill of Rights was written after the Declaration of Independence.	Word: powers Definition: Sentence:
Word: Constitution Definition: Sentence:	Word: protect Definition: Sentence:
Word: delegate Definition: Sentence:	Word: retain Definition: Sentence:
Word: guarantee Definition: Sentence:	Word: right Definition: Sentence:
Word: liberty Definition: Sentence:	Word: wisely penned Definition: Sentence:

© Hampton-Brown

We the People . . .

Washington, D.C. has many beautiful buildings; nevertheless, the Capitol Building commands attention.

> ## Compound Sentences
>
> A **conjunctive adverb** often joins two independent clauses in a compound sentence. Use a semicolon before the conjunctive adverb and a comma after it.
>
> The Constitution is the highest law in the United States; **therefore**, the American people respect it.

DIRECTIONS Work with a partner. Use a dictionary to find the meanings of the conjunctive adverbs. Then write the conjunctive adverb that best completes each sentence. Use correct punctuation.

Some Conjunctive Adverbs
consequently
nevertheless
meanwhile
then
thus
besides
therefore
however
moreover

1. The American colonies had strong economies of their own in the 1760's _; however,_ _____ they were ruled by England.

2. England needed money to support its empire_____ the colonists had to pay more taxes.

3. The taxes were not very heavy at first_____ the colonists resented "taxation without representation."

4. King George wanted the colonists to provide housing for his troops _____ the British passed an act to make the colonists provide free lodging.

5. Many colonists were angry about the new laws_____ they were tired of British rule.

6. Some people started holding secret meetings_____ others were collecting weapons.

7. The colonies lacked a great army_____ they went to war.

8. The British saw defeat ahead_____ they signed a peace treaty.

9. The colonists wanted a new and fair system of government_____ they wrote the Constitution to establish the main laws of the country.

10. The new country created three branches of government_____ one branch cannot gain too much power.

GRAMMAR: COMPLEX SENTENCES

Rights and Wrongs

DIRECTIONS Work with a group. Review each amendment. What would happen if this amendment did not exist? Discuss your ideas. Then add a clause to complete the sentence.

Complex Sentences

A **complex sentence** has one independent clause and one or more dependent clauses. In some complex sentences, **if** introduces the dependent clause and **then** introduces the independent clause.

If the Constitution did not have the Bill of Rights, **then** Americans would not have many liberties.

☆ **Amendment 1** If people could not say what they

think, then _they could not criticize the government_ .

☆ **Amendment 2** If people could not protect themselves from harm, then _____

_____ .

☆ **Amendment 3** _____ ,

then soldiers could come and live in your house without your permission.

☆ **Amendment 4** _____ ,

then innocent people would be jailed.

☆ **Amendment 5** If a person could be tried twice for the same crime, then _____

_____ .

☆ **Amendment 6** _____ ,

then the person could be kept in jail indefinitely.

☆ **Amendment 7** _____ ,

then the person could be unfairly convicted.

☆ **Amendment 8** If fines and punishments were unreasonable, then _____

_____ .

☆ **Amendment 9** If Amendment 9 didn't exist, then _____

_____ .

☆ **Amendment 10** If the states had no powers, then _____

_____ .

Connect New Information

DIRECTIONS Follow the steps to make and use a K-W-L Chart.

1 Preview the article.

The Electoral College

Elector Barbara Simmons
certifies her vote.
December, 2000

When most voters cast their ballots in a presidential election, they think that they are voting for the President and the Vice President. This is not exactly true, however. Their ballots actually elect members of the electoral college who represent the voters.

The electoral college is the constitutional system for the election of the President and Vice President of the United States. Electors pledge to support the candidates the voters of their state chose. This means that the electors agree to cast their votes for Candidate X, if the voters of their state chose that candidate. In this way, the electoral college represents the voters.

The electors vote in December of each presidential election year. Their votes elect the next President and Vice President.

2 Use a K-W-L chart to show what you already know and want to learn.

K What I **K**now	W What I **W**ant to Learn	L What I **L**earned

3 Go back and read the article carefully. Add what you learn to the chart.

4 Tell a partner what you learned about the electoral college. Discuss any questions you still have about the topic.

GRAMMAR: INDEFINITE PRONOUNS

Auditions Tonight!

DIRECTIONS Finish the announcement.
Use words from the box.

anybody	everybody	somebody	nobody
anyone	everyone	someone	no one
anything	everything	something	nothing

Indefinite Pronouns

When you are not talking about a specific person or thing, use an **indefinite pronoun**. When a singular indefinite pronoun is the subject of the sentence, use a singular verb.

Everybody is going to the audition.
Nothing keeps them away!

Auditions Tonight!

If you have _____nothing_____ to do tonight, why not try out for "The Bill of Rights
                    1.

Rap"? _____ is welcome. Just be sure you know _____
              2.   **3.**

about the Bill of Rights. _____ will expect you to recite all ten amendments.
                                  4.

However, the lyrics explain the Bill of Rights, so _____ you know will
                                                            5.

be helpful.

_____ who is interested should come to the auditorium at 7:00 p.m.
        6.

_____ will be there to let you in. _____ will have time to read
        7.   **8.**

the lyrics and practice. The auditions start at 8:00 p.m. _____ should get
                                                                    9.

nervous! _____ will go wrong.
              10.

Although _____ will try out with a mike, bring
                11.

your best rap voice. That's _____ , except—come
                                    12.

with plenty of enthusiasm. After all, this is the Bill of Rights!

MORE ABOUT INDEFINITE PRONOUNS Write a paragraph telling what happened
at the audition. Use indefinite pronouns.

© Hampton-Brown

WRITING: A PUBLIC SERVICE ANNOUNCEMENT

For Your Information...

DIRECTIONS Choose one of the freedoms defined in the First Amendment. Write a public service announcement about it.

1 **Plan the announcement.**

• Choose which freedom to write about.

• List what you want to say. You might want to use a main idea and details map like the one on Handbook page 374 to show your ideas.

2 **Write the announcement.**

Public Service Announcement

A **public service announcement** is a short message that gives information about an important event or issue. It can appear on TV, on the radio, or in a magazine.

Sutterville City Council Meeting

City Hall, 6 P.M. Tues., June 17

The council will discuss the proposal to build a hotel on Ocean Street. City residents are invited to voice their opinions about this project. Call the City Clerk at 555-0862 for more information.

Write a title that names the topic.

_____

The First Amendment in the Bill of Rights gives us the right to _____

Describe what rights the freedom gives every American. Explain how the freedom affects people.

_____ .

This means that _____

_____ .

This freedom is important because _____

_____ .

Tell your audience about someone they can contact for more information, or tell about a book, an organization, or a Web site.

To find out more about this freedom, contact _____

_____ .

3 **Review the announcement.**

• If you are going to record your announcement, present it as a rap, or read it aloud, ask a partner to listen to your announcement. Your partner can suggest changes to make your writing better.

• Edit and revise your announcement.

4 **Present the announcement.**

Arrange a time to present or display it to your class, school, or community.

The History of Women's Suffrage

DIRECTIONS Review your notes about women's suffrage.
Make an outline. Then write a research report.

For your outline:

Give your report a **title**.
Write the title last, after
you have organized
your ideas.

_____

I. _____

   A. _____

Decide on the **main ideas**
you will cover. Write
each main idea after a
Roman numeral.

      1. _____

      2. _____

Find details to go with
each main idea. Each
detail follows a capital
letter. Each **related detail**
follows a number.

   B. _____

      1. _____

      2. _____

      3. _____

II. _____

   A. _____

   B. _____

      1. _____

      2. _____

III. _____

   A. _____

   B. _____

For your report:

1. Write the title from your outline.

2. Turn each main idea with a Roman numeral into a topic sentence
   for a paragraph. Turn the details and related details into sentences
   that tell more about each main idea.

3. Edit and revise your report. Then present your report in an
   interesting way.

1913: A suffragette parade
in New York City

Words About Slaves and Laws

New Words

abolitionist

captivity

case

defense

deliberate

illegal

legal

prisoner

slave trader

slavery

Relate Words

DIRECTIONS Write the new words in the correct categories.

Law Words	Slavery Words
_____	_____
_____	_____
_____	_____
_____	_____

Use New Words in Context

DIRECTIONS Write the new words to complete the paragraph.

The practice of _____ began early in America's history.
1.

Africans were brought to Virginia and held in _____ .
2.

A _____ would then sell his African _____ .
3.   4.

In 1777, Vermont made slavery _____ .
5.

The _____ fought to end slavery in all of
6.

the U. S. By 1808, it was no longer _____
7.

to import slaves, but you could still own them. In a famous

court _____ , a slave named Dred Scott
8.

A slave auction in
Virginia, 1861.

sued for his freedom. His _____ was that if
9.

he moved to a free state, he should be a free man. However, the Supreme

Court met to _____ and ruled against Scott.
10.

With a Twist

DIRECTIONS Learn about irony. Follow the steps.

1 **Read the first paragraph of the story.**

> **Irony**
>
> **Irony** is when an event or circumstance in life or literature does not match what we expect.
>
> *Amistad* means "friendship" in Spanish. The name is ironic because the ship was not a friendly place.

Marvelous Ms. Marvel

We sat around the dinner table finalizing the plans for our club's awards ceremony. Ms. Marvel, as usual, had set the tone. Her taste was impeccable and we all secretly watched her to see what was proper in any social situation.

---

2 **Answers the questions.**

1. Why do the club members feel that Ms. Marvel is marvelous? _____

_____

2. What do you expect will happen in the story? _____

_____

3 **Read the rest of the story.**

> When it was time for dessert, Connie served her homemade sponge cake with an absolutely delicious sauce. As we finished off the cake, the sounds of spoons scraping plates could be heard around the room. We all loved that sauce! Several of us even thought of licking our plates just to get one last taste of the ambrosia. We would never do it, though. We would not want to shame Ms. Marvel.
>
> Suddenly Ms. Marvel sighed and shook her head with a strange dissatisfied expression. Then she looked around quickly, shrugged her perfect shoulders, and put down her spoon. Raising her plate ever so delicately to her lips, Ms. Marvel proceeded to lick every drop of sauce from it. Then she smiled and said, in her most ladylike tones, "Now <u>that</u> was an excellent dessert!" The short, stunned silence that followed was shattered by shrieks of delight. Ms. Marvel had led the way again!

4 **Discuss the irony with a partner. Explain what was ironic about Ms. Marvel's actions.**

Beliefs That Matter!

Lewis Tappan was a successful businessman who worked courageously for the abolition of slavery.

> **Relative Clauses**
>
> A **relative clause** is one kind of dependent clause used in a complex sentence. It tells more about a person or thing. A relative clause begins with a **relative pronoun**.
>
> Tappan was a man **who believed slavery was wrong.**

DIRECTIONS Underline the relative clause in each sentence. Write the relative pronoun. Then circle the noun that the relative clause tells more about.

Relative Pronoun

1. Lewis Tappan was an (abolitionist) who helped Cinqué and other Africans.   who

2. Tappan, whose family was very religious, was born in Massachusetts in 1788. _____

3. At sixteen, he started work in a store that sold dry goods. _____

4. Later, he joined his brother in a business, which was called Arthur Tappan and Company. _____

5. Tappan was a person who cared about other human beings. _____

6. He was also a man that acted on his beliefs. _____

7. Lewis Tappan held beliefs that others opposed, but he had the courage to speak out. _____

8. In 1833, he and his brother, who shared his beliefs, formed a group to fight slavery. _____

9. They also wanted to help people that were not free. _____

10. The group, which was called the Anti-Slavery Society, had an impact. _____

11. Cinqué and the other Africans were people whom Tappan helped. _____

12. He visited the Africans who were in prison. _____

13. Tappan figured out the legal strategy that was used in their trials. _____

14. After the trial, it was Tappan who helped Cinqué and his companions get home to Sierra Leone. _____

© Hampton-Brown

GRAMMAR: COMPLEX SENTENCES

A Man to Remember

DIRECTIONS Work with a partner. Underline the independent clause in each sentence. Circle the dependent clause or clauses. Then write the subordinating conjunctions and relative pronouns in the chart.

1. (When Cinqué was captured,) he was a farmer (who grew rice.)

2. He was a married man in his twenties whose father was a local chief.

3. After he was captured, slavers changed his name, which had been Sengbe Pieh.

4. Cinqué endured many hardships while he was on the *Amistad.*

5. When the situation became unbearable, Cinqué led the revolt that occurred on the ship.

6. Although Cinqué was finally able to go home, he discovered awful news.

7. Wars had killed his family whom he had not seen for three years.

8. We don't know what happened to the man who led a revolt for freedom.

9. There are no reports of him after he traveled down the coast where he became a trader.

10. Because Cinqué was a man whose courage inspired others, he will always be remembered.

> **Complex Sentences**
>
> A **complex sentence** may have more than one dependent clause.
>
> A **relative clause** is one kind of dependent clause. It begins with a **relative pronoun**.
>
> Joseph Cinqué was the man **who led the revolt**.
>
> Other dependent clauses begin with **subordinating conjunctions**.
>
> **After the revolt**, Cinqué took charge.
>
> Sometimes both kinds of dependent clauses are used in one sentence.
>
> **Before Joseph Cinqué was captured**, he lived in a town called Mani, **which was near the coast of Sierra Leone**.

"We have done no wrong."

Subordinating Conjunctions	Relative Pronouns
when	who

Name _____   Date _____

SUM IT UP

Relate Causes and Effects

DIRECTIONS Read Clara's report about the abolitionist movement. Then complete the cause–and–effect chart.

The Abolitionist Movement

Abolitionists believed it was wrong for one human being to own another. They wanted to abolish slavery in the United States.

In the 1830s, Charles Finney and other preachers gave speeches about freeing the slaves. Arthur and Lewis Tappan agreed with Finney's message. With William Lloyd Garrison, they organized the American Anti-Slavery Society in 1833.

Because of the Society's publications and speeches, the abolitionist movement gained support from some members of Congress. After the Civil War started, abolitionists and some members of Congress convinced President Lincoln to sign the Emancipation Proclamation. This freed slaves in many states. A few years later, Congress passed the Thirteenth Amendment, which freed all the slaves in the United States. The abolitionists had succeeded.

Cause: Charles Finney and other preachers gave speeches about freeing the slaves.

Effect: The Tappan brothers and William Lloyd Garrison agreed with Finney's message.

Effect:

Effect:

Effect:

Effect:

GRAMMAR: RELATIVE PRONOUNS

He Fought for Freedom

DIRECTIONS Complete each sentence with a relative pronoun from the box.

that	who	whom	whose

> **Relative Pronouns**
>
> A **relative pronoun** introduces a relative clause. Use **who, whom,** or **whose** for people. Use **that** for people or things.
>
> Cinqué was a man **who wanted freedom.**
>
> *Amistad* was a ship **that became famous.**

1. *Amistad* was a ship _____that_____ carried slaves.

2. Cinqué was a man _____ was kidnapped by slave traders.

3. This man _____ fought for freedom was courageous.

4. Cinqué was taken from the people _____ he loved.

5. The name _____ he was given as a child was changed.

6. He and many other Africans were placed on a ship _____ was headed for Cuba.

7. Cinqué led a revolt against the men _____ kidnapped him.

8. He was a leader _____ bravery inspired others.

9. Cinqué and the other slaves _____ took over the *Amistad* wanted to sail back to Africa.

10. Instead, the ship _____ they seized drifted into the harbor of New London, Connecticut.

11. The Africans, _____ were tired and weary, were sent to prison.

12. In prison, Cinqué met abolitionists _____ hard work helped free him and the others.

13. John Quincy Adams, _____ was a former president, also fought for the Africans.

14. In court, he gave a speech _____ lasted more than eight hours.

15. The Africans, _____ dream was to be free, were finally released.

Joseph Cinqué is the name that was given to Sengbe Pieh by the slave traders who took him from his land. This is how one artist believes he may have looked as he stood before the court.

MORE ABOUT RELATIVE PRONOUNS Write complex sentences about a person you admire. Include some relative clauses. Circle the relative pronouns.

Using the Internet

DIRECTIONS How do you use a search engine? Answer the questions. For tips on using the Internet, see pages 47, 392, and 393 in your book.

1. What is a search engine? *It is an on-line service that you can use to find information on the Internet.*

2. Each search engine has its own Web site. How do you go to a specific search engine? _____ _____

3. What is the first thing you do to find information with a search engine? _____

4. What do you do next? _____ _____

5. How do you go to a Web site that the search engine has found? _____

6. What do you do when you find a useful Web site? _____ _____

Search Engine

Search engines are on-line services that you can use to find information on the Internet. When you enter key words, a search engine shows a list of Web sites that have those words in them.

A search engine home page might look like this.

DIRECTIONS Work with a partner. Use a search engine to learn about the African slave trade that brought Africans to North America.

7. Write information about your search.

   search engine address: _____

   key words: _____

8. Write the address of a useful Web site you found. Describe the information it has.

   Tell about the topics, graphics, and links. _____ _____ _____ _____

Compare Paths to Freedom

DIRECTIONS Work with a group. Compare the experiences of Cinqué and the runaway slaves who used the Underground Railroad.

1 **Start a Comparison Chart** Write what you know about Cinqué. Include the answers to questions such as:

- What might happen to Cinqué if he failed to accomplish his goal?
- Who helped him? What did they do?
- Did Cinqué use the law, or break it?
- Where did Cinqué want to go?

Cinqué	Runaway Slaves
a slave waiting in prison	slaves on the run
wanted freedom	wanted freedom

2 **Research the Underground Railroad** Use the Internet, encyclopedias, and other sources. Find information about the runaway slaves to add to the chart. Look for answers to the same questions you asked about Cinqué.

3 **Review Your Chart** In your group, discuss the similarities and differences between the experiences of the runaway slaves and Cinqué.

4 **Present Your Findings** Share your ideas with the class. Did other groups reach the same conclusions?

In Your Mind's Eye

DIRECTIONS Have a partner read the poem. Close your eyes and visualize the scene. Then draw a picture.

Visualize

When you **visualize**, you use one or more of your five senses to make a picture, or **sensory image**, in your mind.

School Lunchroom
— SweetP

Steam rising from plastic trays,
Fresh tuna salad,
Stale hot dogs,
Warm tortillas,
Sweet apples,
Salty peanuts,
Spicy salsa,
Crisp chips,
Cool soda,
Cherry pie,
Rattling bags,
Colorful jackets,
Hundreds of voices shouting.
Ah, the peace of our midday break!

Visualization

DIRECTIONS Write the details from the poem that go with each sense.

Sense	Sensory Details
Sight	steam rising from plastic trays,
Touch	warm tortillas,
Smell	
Taste	
Sound	

MORE ABOUT VISUALIZATION Visualize a new situation. Use details for each of the five senses to describe it. Share your description with a partner.

BUILD LANGUAGE AND VOCABULARY

Show You Care!

DIRECTIONS Read the persuasive speech. Underline each verb that is in the present perfect tense.

❝Our community needs to start a program to beautify our streets. Many streets have grown cluttered and shabby-looking. The city has allowed public buildings and parks to deteriorate. We have seen trash build up along our roads.

I have thought about ways to beautify our streets, and I have spoken to people at City Hall. The city council has assured me that they will give us money for paint and other supplies. They have promised the money if we supply the volunteers. They have agreed to purchase trees, hanging flower baskets, and new trash containers. The mayor has appeared on TV about it.

I have also encouraged businesses to get involved. One restaurant has offered to set up an outdoor café. A row of shops has organized to create a bike path. A local artist has made sketches of what a new downtown might look like.

I have decided to do as much as I can to help beautify our town. What about you? Will you volunteer?❞

Present Perfect Tense

The **present perfect tense** can tell about an action that happened in the past, but the exact time is not known.

The city **has made** many improvements.

It uses **has** or **have** followed by the **past participle** of the verb. Regular past participles end in **-ed**. Irregular past participles vary in their forms.

Businesses **have painted** their store fronts.
Many people **have shown** that they care.

Beautification projects in other cities have encouraged many people to spend time downtown on weekends.

DIRECTIONS Work in a group to write a song of triumph! Think about a change you'd like to make. Pretend that you have made it happen. Include some verbs in the present perfect tense.

Example:

> **Winds of Change**
>
> We have made it happen!
> I have seen the change!
> Look out on the hillsides.
> Turbines spin and whirl.
> The wind has fueled our homes and shops.
> The winds of change have started.
> Our future has begun.

_____

_____

_____

_____

_____

_____

_____

_____

_____

Name _____ Date _____

Words About Conflict

New Words

conflict
consensus
diffuse
dispute
intervene
mediation
negotiation
peer
resolution

Identify Synonyms

DIRECTIONS Write a new word next to its synonym.

Synonym	New Words
weaken	
discussion	
decision	
quarrel	
equal	
agreement	

Use New Words in Context

DIRECTIONS Use the new words to complete the word map.
Some words may be used more than once.

What is it?
It is a process of resolving
_____ through
_____ .

What are examples?
Having a friend
_____
to help settle an argument
with another friend.

peer mediation

What can it accomplish?
It can help _____
or _____ .
Both parties can reach a
_____
and resolve a
_____ .

© Hampton-Brown

GRAMMAR: TRANSITIVE AND INTRANSITIVE VERBS

Man of Steel

Christopher Reeve, who was paralyzed in a riding accident, hopes to walk again one day.

Transitive and Intransitive Verbs

A **transitive verb** needs an object to complete its meaning. The **object** answers the question *Whom?* or *What?*

Christopher Reeve **inspires** people.
Whom or what does Christopher Reeve inspire?
He inspires **people**.

An **intransitive verb** does not need an object to complete its meaning.
He **works** for good causes.

DIRECTIONS Circle the verb in each sentence. Say the verb and ask, *Whom?* or *What?* to decide if there is an object. Underline the object if there is one. Then write *transitive* or *intransitive*.

Type of Verb

1. In 1978, Christopher Reeve (made) a <u>movie</u> about Superman.   _____transitive_____

2. The film turned Reeve into a star.   _____

3. In real life, Reeve acted like a super man, too.   _____

4. He loved sports.   _____

5. He flew his own plane.   _____

6. He skied with his family.   _____

7. He rode horses competitively.   _____

8. In 1995, Reeve broke his neck in a riding accident.   _____

9. The accident paralyzed his body from the neck down.   _____

10. Today, Reeve helps other people with spinal-cord injuries.   _____

11. He raises money for medical research.   _____

12. He meets with scientists.   _____

13. He sets goals for the future.   _____

14. Reeve still works on movies.   _____

15. He lives optimistically.   _____

A Solution That Works

Relative Pronouns

A **relative pronoun** begins a relative clause. A **relative clause** is one kind of dependent clause. It tells more about a person or thing.

Use **which** for things. Separate the clause from the rest of the sentence with commas.

The session, **which I attended**, was helpful.

José wanted Katrina to listen, **which she did**.

Use **that** for people or things. Do not use commas to separate a clause beginning with **that**.

The solution **that we found** was popular.

DIRECTIONS Underline the relative clause in each sentence. Circle the relative pronoun.

1. The mediator explains the rules (that) will guide the session.

2. Honest expression, which is part of the process, is necessary.

3. Participants explain the problem that needs mediation.

4. Name-calling and teasing, which are very hurtful, can lead to difficult mediation sessions.

5. In the end, people that once felt resentment may become friends.

6. The contract, which everyone signs, is an important final step.

DIRECTIONS Read each pair of sentences. Combine the sentences using *which* or *that*.

7. Two students had a problem. The problem required peer mediation. (**that**)

   Two students had a problem (that) required peer mediation.

   _____

8. Several students offered their help. They believed in peer mediation. (**that**)

   _____

   _____

9. José and Katrina's problem was difficult. It involved hurt feelings. (**which**)

   _____

   _____

10. The peer mediation session found a solution. The solution satisfied Katrina and José. (**that**)

   _____

   _____

© Hampton-Brown

Something to Talk About

DIRECTIONS Complete each sentence. Use the present perfect tense of the verb in parentheses. See Handbook pages 450–451 for a list of irregular past participles.

> ### Present Perfect Tense
>
> The **present perfect tense** can tell about an action that happened in the past, but the exact time is not known. It can also tell about an action that began in the past and may still be going on.
>
> It uses **has** or **have** followed by the **past participle**. The verb agrees with the subject.
>
> Parisa **has heard** about mediation.
> She and her friends **have discussed** it.

1. Parisa _____has decided_____ to try peer mediation. (**decide**)

2. Something _____ that she wants to resolve. (**happen**)

3. For several weeks, she _____ part of a group in science class. (**be**)

4. Some of the group members _____ to get out of the work. (**try**)

5. They _____ most of the project to Parisa. (**leave**)

6. This situation _____ Parisa really angry. (**make**)

7. She _____ everyone to come to a peer mediation session. (**ask**)

8. All the group members _____ to participate. (**agree**)

9. The mediators _____ a date and a time. (**arrange**)

10. Parisa _____ about how she will explain her position. (**think**)

11. She _____ nervous about it, though. (**feel**)

12. Her parents _____ her that she is doing the right thing. (**tell**)

MORE ABOUT THE PRESENT PERFECT TENSE Write sentences using verbs in the present perfect tense. Use the past participles of these verbs: *become, give, bring, know, mean,* and *sing.*

Students resolve a conflict in a peer mediation session.

© Hampton-Brown

Name _____ Date _____

Compare and Evaluate

DIRECTIONS Compare the article "Dealing with Conflict," with the letters to the editor on pages 192–193 of your book. Complete the chart.

	Article	Letters to the Editor
Purpose		
Facts: A <u>fact</u> is a statement that can be proven.	definitions of conflict	Jan experienced peer mediation.
Opinions: An <u>opinion</u> is what a person feels or thinks.	Katrina didn't think José looked right for the part.	Peer mediation teaches students to take responsibility. Jan thinks Robert thinks

MORE ABOUT EVALUATING LITERATURE Choose the article or one of the letters. Write a paragraph that evaluates how well the author met the purpose for writing. Use information in the chart.

Put the Pieces Together

DIRECTIONS Work with a partner to learn about seven kinds of context clues.

1 Discuss the chart. Tell how each sample sentence illustrates the context clue.

Type of Clue and What It Does	Sample Sentence
An **appositive** comes right after a word and defines or describes it. It is usually set off by commas or parentheses.	The proscenium, **the part of the stage in front of the curtain,** was lit by two green spotlights.
A **contrast** clue helps you understand a new word by showing you its opposite or how it is different.	The theater was hushed **until** the curtain rose and **jungle sounds broke the silence.**
A **description** clue creates a word picture of an unfamiliar word.	For a backdrop, **the stage wall was painted green, with thin swirls of white, like mist.**
An **example** clue lists one kind, or several kinds, of something.	Props **such as tall trees, hanging vines, and a river of blue cloth,** made the stage look like a jungle.
A passage uses a **definition** clue when it states the meaning of the word.	The tech crew **is the team that operates the lights and sounds. They also move things around on stage.**
An **explanation** clue helps you understand a new word by telling you more about it.	A sound technician **broadcasts bird calls and the sound of rain from several speakers.**
A **restatement** clue follows a new word; it says the same thing again using different words.	When the play was over, there was thunderous applause. **The clapping was as loud as thunder!**

2 **Circle the kind of context clue used in each sentence.**

1. Peer mediation can help friends <u>reconcile</u>. **It can restore friendship and bring harmony.**

   appositive
   (restatement)

2. In mediation, participants need good <u>listening skills</u>, **such as eye contact and repeating what they hear to check accuracy**.

   example
   contrast

3. The two girls here on Tuesday were so <u>distraught</u> **that their words came out jumbled, and they cried.**

   contrast
   description

4. **It would have been wrong for anyone to tell what happened during the session** because there is a rule of <u>confidentiality</u>.

   definition
   explanation

5. The girls signed a <u>contract</u>. A contract **is a written agreement.**

   definition
   example

6. The two girls left the room feeling <u>serene</u>, **not distraught.**

   contrast
   restatement

7. The <u>arbitrators</u>, **the people who mediate the dispute**, left the room feeling successful.

   example
   appositive

3 **The italicized word in each sentence is a nonsense word. Underline the context clues that help you interpret its meaning. Write a definition for each nonsense word.**

Definition

8. The people of the planet Marab discovered a new moon. They had a *fribjab* <u>because they couldn't agree</u> about what to do with the moon.

   <u>conflict, disagreement, dispute</u>

   _____

9. The Daps wanted to turn the moon into a beautiful *rizl*, with trees, benches, and playgrounds.

   _____

   _____

10. The Zems wanted to put up a lot of large *zigwids*, like shops, banks, and apartments.

    _____

    _____

11. The mediator helped the Daps and Zems *perdol*, or talk back and forth, about their ideas.

    _____

    _____

12. At last they came to a *nildop*. They were all satisfied with the final decision.

    _____

    _____

Analyzing Arguments

DIRECTIONS With a group, study the information in the box. Then discuss the letters to the editor on pages 192-193 in your book. Which weaknesses does each letter have? Complete the chart.

Analyzing Arguments

An **argument** gives an opinion about a topic. When you **analyze** an argument, consider weaknesses that make it less believable or unreliable.

Argument Weaknesses

Missing Information Not all of the facts are presented. The writer may give only two ways to solve a problem, when there are actually four ways.

Inaccurate Information The information is wrong. The writer may say that the teacher assigned the peer mediators, when they actually volunteered.

Faulty Facts There are mistakes about numbers or places. The writer may say that peer mediators helped in 5 cases, when they actually helped in 10.

Biased Opinion One viewpoint is favored over another. The writer may have only good things to say about the topic and not mention negative aspects.

Exaggeration Making something seem more important than it is. Saying that peer mediation helped every student in the school would be an exaggeration.

Argument Weaknesses	Examples in Jan's letter	Examples in Robert's letter
missing information	gives only two ways to handle student conflicts	
inaccurate information		
faulty facts		
biased opinions		
exaggerations		

What Does It Really Mean?

DIRECTIONS Read the ad. Then read each description. Tell whether it describes an apparent agenda or a hidden agenda.

> ## Apparent and Hidden Agendas
>
> The **apparent agenda** is stated directly. It could be something for people to see or to do.
>
> The **hidden agenda** is not stated directly. It is a way to get the reader to think about a person, product, or company.

Come to the Game!

The Pine Woods Patriots will play their first game on May 4 at 2 p.m. at the Pine Park Field. Join us in supporting our new team. Show our kids you care!

Ad and team shirts paid for by Anderson Home Repair.

1. The Anderson Home Repair Company takes out an ad and buys shirts to show their support of the team.

   _____

2. The Anderson Home Repair Company advertises its business in the ad and on the t-shirts. People who see that the company is doing something good for the community will probably want to use its services.

   _____

DIRECTIONS Read the script from a TV commercial. Identify the apparent and hidden agendas.

> "This Saturday, come and help us celebrate our 10th year in business at Finkleberry Toy Store! Joey Rizzo, star of the hit TV series *Space Rangers*, will be here to sign autographs. Kids will get free balloons and party favors, and the first 100 people that come will each receive a free Tiny Tad Teddy Bear! The party is on Saturday, June 14th, from 10 a.m. to 2 p.m. at our store in the Sunny Ridge Mall. Don't miss the fun!"

3. What is the apparent agenda? _____

   _____

4. What is the hidden agenda? _____

   _____

CONTENT AREA CONNECTIONS

Write About the United Nations

DIRECTIONS Read the definitions for the words in the box.
Use the words to complete the sentences. Then use three of
the words to write your own sentences.

This is the symbol for the United Nations.
One of the main roles of the
organization is to mediate
disagreements among nations.

> **Terms Related to Conflict and Mediation**
> - **aggression** a movement in the direction of a fight
> - **diplomacy** the skill of helping others get along
> - **disarmament** stopping the use of weapons in a conflict
> - **dispute** a disagreement or argument between two people or groups
> - **peacekeeping** keeping the peace
> - **reconciliation** helping parties in a disagreement get back together
> - **violence** aggression that causes injury

1. The United Nations helps groups avoid conflict through ___peacekeeping___ .

2. Many times, two countries will have a _____ about
   borders or trade agreements.

3. One country might commit an act of _____ , such as taking
   over part of another country. This could lead to a fight between the two nations.

4. If the aggression turns into _____ , innocent people
   may be injured or killed.

5. The U.N. will send in experts who are trained in _____
   to help the two groups find a way to get along.

6. These experts help negotiate a _____ which brings the
   groups back together.

7. The U.N. tries to get the groups to agree to a _____
   so that weapons will not be used.

8. _____

   _____

9. _____

   _____

10. _____

    _____

RESEARCH SKILLS

How to Use an Almanac

DIRECTIONS Study the sample home page and article from an on-line almanac. Then answer the questions.

Almanac

An **almanac** is a reference book that gives facts about a variety of topics. It has tables, lists, diagrams, and special features that provide information. It is updated each year. An **on-line almanac** has similar facts and features, but it is easier to use because you can quickly find information by typing in key words.

To find an **on-line almanac**, use a search engine. The home page might look like this.

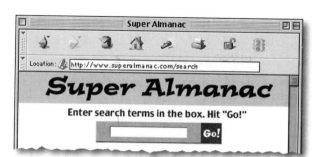

An article might look like this.

Links are underlined. Click on a link to go to an article about a related topic.

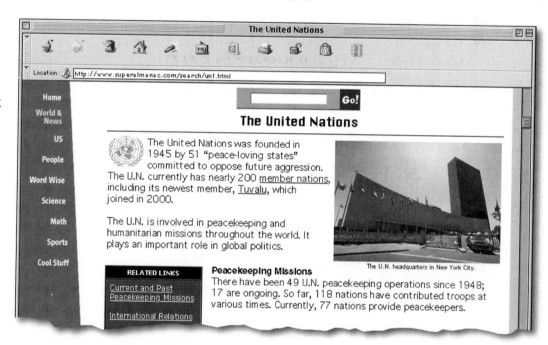

1. What key words would you enter to find this article? _____

2. What kinds of missions does the U.N. engage in? _____

_____

3. How do you know if there is an article about a related topic? _____

_____

4. How do you go to one of the related articles? _____

5. Under which heading can you find out how many nations currently provide

   troops for U.N. missions? _____

Legal Words

Use New Words in Context

New Words

- false accusation
- falsely arrested
- inconvenient
- merchandise
- misconstrue
- possession
- publicly humiliated
- security guard
- shoplifter
- unrighteousness

DIRECTIONS Use the new words to complete the dialogue. Then act out the scenes with a partner.

Scene A:

You: Excuse me, is this _merchandise_____

on sale today?

Saleswoman: No, it isn't. You have _unrighteousness_____

the ad. The sale is next week.

You: Oh, no! I rushed all the way here, and now I'll have to come back.

How very _inconvenient_____!

Saleswoman: I'm very sorry for your trouble.

Scene B:

Security Guard: Why do you have that bracelet in your

_possession_____? It looks like you

are a _shoplifter_____.

Young Woman: I am not! That is a _merchandise_____

I am trying to return this because it doesn't fit.

Security Guard: A likely story. You're under arrest.

Young Woman: Here's my sales receipt. I protest the

_publicely humilated_____ of this. I have

been _falsly arrested_____

and _falsef accusation_____.

Security Guard: Okay. Calm down. Let's see what the salesperson says.

MORE VOCABULARY Work with a partner. Pick five new words. Have your partner paraphrase definitions for each word without looking at the book.

GRAMMAR: HELPING VERBS

Shopping Day

DIRECTIONS Circle the helping verb in the first sentence. Write what the sentence means. Then add a different helping verb to the second sentence and write what the new sentence means.

Helping Verbs
Some verbs are made up of more than one word. The verb that comes before the main verb is the **helping verb**.
  Yoko **will buy** a dress.

1. Yoko (can) go shopping.

   Yoko is able to go shopping.

   Yoko ____will____ go shopping.

   Yoko plans to go shopping.

Helping Verb	Meaning
can	you are able to
may	you have permission to
will	it is a future plan or possibility
must	you are required to

2. Yoko must spend her own money.

   _____

   _____

   Yoko _____ spend her own money.

   _____

3. Yoko will go to a big department store.

   _____

   Yoko _____ go to a big department store.

   _____

4. Yoko may take a taxi home.

   _____

   Yoko _____ take a taxi home.

   _____

5. Yoko can share her new things with her sister.

   _____

   Yoko _____ share her new things with her sister.

   _____

Stylish Writing

DIRECTIONS Work with a group to complete the chart for "The Truth About Sharks." Would you call Joan Bauer's style fast–moving, lively, comic, or realistic? Write a sentence explaining the group's choice.

Elements of Style

Style is an author's unique way of writing. An author's style might be called comic, poetic, serious, scientific, or fast–moving.

To create a style, authors use various techniques, such as:
• vivid descriptions
• lively dialogue
• showing rather than telling

Elements of Style	Story Examples	How the Element Helps Me Understand
Descriptions What descriptive words paint clear pictures?	funeral gray nearly dropped her fangs	The security guard seems mean and unfriendly.
Dialogue What characters' words help you understand their actions?	"Ma'am, I'm innocent," I said.	
Showing Rather Than Telling How does the author show the characters' actions and feelings?	A cold fear swept through me.	

_____

_____

_____

Relate Problems and Solutions

DIRECTIONS Read the story and complete the problem–and–solution chart.

Gargi's Pets

All her life Gargi had wanted a dog. When her family moved to a big house from their apartment, she was sure she'd get her wish.

"Please, Mom, you know how much I want a dog."

"Yes, I know, Gargi, and I was hoping we could say yes, but I got some disappointing news yesterday," her mom told her. "The doctor did some tests, and I'm allergic to cats and dogs. I'm afraid we just can't have any furry pets."

Gargi decided to conduct some research. She went to a pet store. She saw snakes and iguanas, but they needed a lot of special equipment. Finally, Gargi got some fish. They were beautiful, but she couldn't play with them.

"How about a guinea pig?" asked her friend, Jorge.

"Nope." sighed Gargi. "Fur," she and Jorge said together.

One day Gargi was playing with her neighbor's cats. Suddenly she had a bright idea. She would start a dog-sitting business. She could walk dogs and play with them when their owners were away. Now Gargi has lots of dogs—and gets paid for having fun!

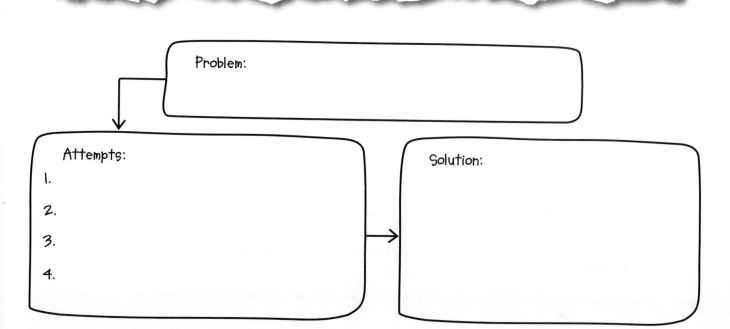

Problem:

Attempts:

1.

2.

3.

4.

Solution:

MORE ABOUT PROBLEMS AND SOLUTIONS Use your chart to write a summary of the story.

An Amazing Bazaar

DIRECTIONS Complete the passage. Write the present perfect tense of each verb. See Handbook pages 450–451 for a list of irregular past participles.

The Covered Bazaar is a huge marketplace in

Istanbul, Turkey. Some people _____*have said*_____ that it
                                       1. say

is the world's first shopping mall. Other people

_____ it a city within a city. Built in 1461,
2. call

the Covered Bazaar _____ over the
                          3. expand

The Covered Bazaar in Istanbul, Turkey, has welcomed shoppers for more than 500 years.

centuries. It is a confusing network of streets and passages filled

with thousands of shops. Fires and earthquakes

_____ the bazaar several times, but it has
4. damage

always been rebuilt.

Some shops in the bazaar _____ the same products for many
                                  5. sell

years. They display beautiful Turkish carpets, gold jewelry, and antiques. Other shops

_____ to stock tourist items such as t-shirts and inexpensive
6. begin

knickknacks. Yet one tradition _____ and
                                      7. remain

_____ the spirit of the old bazaar alive. Each street is known for
8. keep

the trade—such as carpet-making or furniture-making—that was originally practiced in

that district.

Name _____   Date _____

Getting to Know Her

Character Sketch
A **character sketch** is a short, vivid description of a person.

DIRECTIONS Follow these steps to write a character sketch.

1 Think about the girl in "The Truth About Sharks." Make a web to show her traits. Include descriptive details.

2 Use the traits in your web to write similes about the girl. For help, review the lesson on page 127 of your book.

  Example: hair as dark as night

_____   _____

_____   _____

3 Use your similes and the details in your web to write a character sketch.

Describe the girl's features like her hair, eyes, and height.

She has _____

and _____ .

She is _____

_____

_____ .

Give examples of what the girl does that makes her special.

I admire the way she _____

_____

and _____

_____ .

Tell what is important to the girl, or what she has strong feelings about.

She believes that _____

_____ .

Describe what the girl does because of what she believes in.

I know this because _____

_____

_____ .

4 Edit your work to make it more interesting. To improve your writing, see Handbook pages 414–423.

5 Read your work in a group. Compare character sketches.

© Hampton-Brown

RESEARCH SKILLS

Using a Thesaurus

DIRECTIONS Study the sample thesaurus entry. Choose one of the other entries and identify its parts.

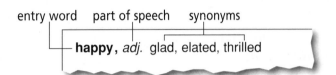

entry word   part of speech   synonyms

happy, *adj.* glad, elated, thrilled

---

run, *verb* race, dart, dash   **shout,** *verb* cry, scream, shriek

scared, *adj.* afraid, frightened, terrified   **take**, *verb* grasp, seize, grab

---

1. entry word: _____

2. part of speech: _____

3. synonyms: _____

DIRECTIONS Replace the word under each line with a synonym. Check a dictionary to make sure you use words with the right meaning.

   Last week I went shopping for clothes at a department store. I was looking at

some shirts when I heard a woman _____ that her little boy was
                                                        4. shout

missing. "I reached over to _____ a sweater from a shelf," she said,
                                              5. take

"and when I turned around, he was gone!" I helped her look for the boy. Suddenly, we

heard a child sobbing. The woman spotted her son standing in the aisle several feet

away. She _____ to him. "I was so _____ ," she
                        6. ran   **7. scared**

said. "I thought I had lost you!" She hugged him because she was so

_____ to have him back.
        8. happy

CONTENT AREA CONNECTIONS

Research Body Chemistry

DIRECTIONS Research and present a visual to show how fear affects the body. Follow the steps.

1 **Plan your research.**

- Where will you look for information? List sources.

☐ Web sites   ☐ books   ☐ other

_____   _____   _____

_____   _____   _____

- What questions do you want to answer? _____

_____

_____

- What key words will you use? _____

2 **Gather information and take notes.**

3 Review your notes. Think of a way to present the information in a visual way. Study these examples and see Handbook pages 370–373 and 390 for more ideas.

Poster

What happens physically during the fight-or-flight reaction?

Brain

Heart

Skin

Chart

Effects of Chronic Stress	
Body System	**Effects**
Circulatory	damaged blood vessels
Immune	weakened resistance to infection

4 **Sketch your idea. Describe what your visual will show.**

_____

_____

_____

_____

_____

5 **Make a final copy of your visual. Then present and explain the results of your research to the class.**

Choices

DIRECTIONS Use the mind map to show some choices people have to make and how difficult the choices might be. As you read the selections in this unit, add more ideas about choices to the map.

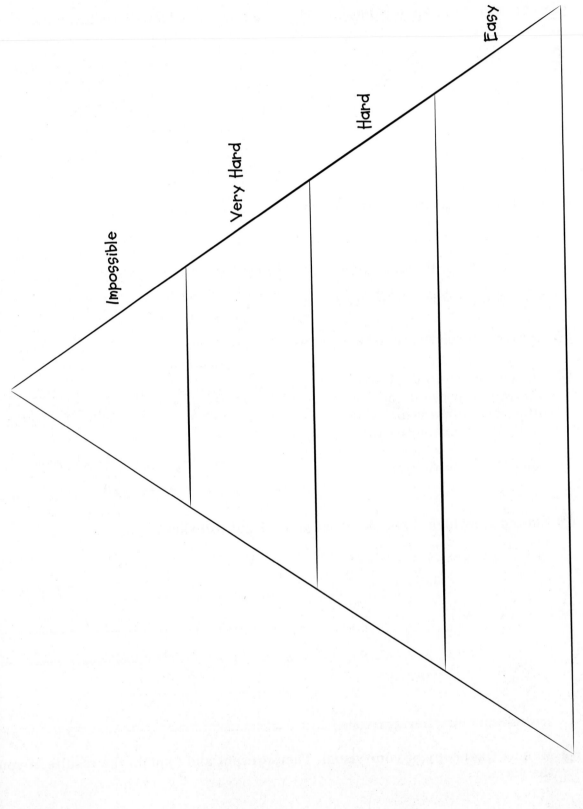

Impossible

Very Hard

Hard

Easy

BUILD LANGUAGE AND VOCABULARY

A King Justifies
His Decisions

DIRECTIONS Read the king's announcement. Circle each verb that is in the past perfect tense.

Past Perfect Tense

The **past tense** tells about an action that happened in the past.

The Deer Prince **presented** himself at the palace.

The **past perfect tense** tells about an action that was completed before some other action in the past. It uses the helping verb **had** followed by the **past participle** of the main verb.

The Deer Prince **had spoken** with the King before.

Loyal Subjects and Deer of the forest,

Before the Deer Prince came to see me, I had killed many deer. Until that time, I had considered the lives of deer unimportant. I had believed that they existed only to please me.

The Deer Prince explained his plan to me. No one had spoken to me like that before! Yet I knew the Deer Prince was right. It would be better to hunt fewer deer. Before the next day dawned, I had decided to accept the Deer Prince's proposal.

A few weeks later, one of my subjects found me in the forest. He had ridden some distance to find me. He had amazing news. The Deer Prince had offered himself for the day's hunt!

I rode swiftly to the palace gates and spoke to the Deer Prince. He explained that he had come to take the place of a pregnant doe. "It is better for one life, rather than two, to be taken," he said.

By that time, my admiration for the Deer Prince had increased greatly. I had acted cruelly and selfishly toward the deer. That is why I make this announcement today. I will kill no more of these fine creatures. From this day forward, they may roam at peace in the royal forest.

MORE ABOUT THE PAST PERFECT TENSE Make a chart of regular and irregular past participles. Begin with past participles from the passage. Add to your chart as you find others in your reading.

Words About a Trial

Paraphrase Definitions

DIRECTIONS Use your own words to write a definition for each new word.

New Words

accused

crime

cruel

guilty

innocent

judge

justice

ordinary

punished

rewarded

1. accused   blamed for something _____

2. crime _____

3. cruel _____

4. guilty _____

5. innocent _____

6. judge _____

7. justice _____

8. ordinary _____

9. punished _____

10. rewarded _____

Use New Words in Context

DIRECTIONS Study the flow chart in your book. Use the new words to write a paragraph that explains the events.

First, someone commits _____

_____

_____

_____

_____

_____

_____

_____

The Lady, or the Tiger?
LEVEL C TE page T224

100

Unit 4 | Choices

GRAMMAR: CONDITIONAL SENTENCES

If He Chooses . . .

DIRECTIONS Complete each sentence. Write a main verb after the underlined helping verb.

> **Conditional Sentences**
>
> A **conditional sentence** tells how one thing depends upon another. It uses helping verbs like **would**, **could**, **can**, **will**, **must**, and **might** before the main verb.
>
> **If** the prisoner is found innocent, he **must marry** the lady behind the door.
>
> Many conditional sentences contain **if** clauses.

1. If the king wanted to, he could _____change_____ the kingdom's system of justice.

2. If the king was fair, he would _____ the young man go.

3. If he is lucky, the young man will _____ the correct door.

4. If he chooses the door with the lady, he may _____ safe.

5. If he chooses the other door, a tiger might _____ him.

_____

DIRECTIONS Complete each sentence. Include a helping verb and main verb.

6. If the young man was brave enough, he _would talk to the king_____

   _____ .

7. If I was the young man, I _____

   _____ .

8. If the princess wants her beloved to live, she _____

   _____ .

9. If the princess's father ruled a country today, he _____

   _____ .

10. If you don't like a country's system of justice, you _____

   _____ .

GRAMMAR: PAST PERFECT TENSE

The Storyteller's Story

Although his father had hoped he would study medicine, Frank Stockton became a writer instead.

Past Perfect Tense

The **past perfect tense** tells about an action that was completed before some other action in the past. It uses the helping verb **had** followed by the **past participle** of the main verb.

> Before I read "The Lady, or the Tiger?," I **had** never **heard** of Frank Stockton.

The **past participle** of regular verbs ends in **-ed**. Irregular past participles vary in their form.

DIRECTIONS Complete the passage. Write the past perfect tense of the verb. See Handbook pages 450–451 for a list of irregular past participles.

Last night I read "The Lady, or the Tiger?" I _____ had heard _____ it before,
                                                                    1. hear

but I _____ how intriguing it is.
                2. forget

The personality of the princess really interests me. The first time I read the story, I

_____ only her good traits. This time, though, I saw that she
          3. notice

was really selfish! By the end of the story, I _____ my
                                        4. reach

conclusion about her sign to her boyfriend.

As I read, I grew curious about the author, Frank Stockton. By nine o'clock, I

_____ some research. Stockton was born in Philadelphia in
        5. do

1834. His father _____ him to study medicine, but he became
                      6. want

an illustrator and writer instead. He wrote "The Lady, or the Tiger?" in the early 1880s.

By the end of his career, he _____ many popular stories, and
                                 7. write

he _____ famous.
     8. become

102

LITERARY ANALYSIS: FORESHADOWING

Think Ahead!

DIRECTIONS Read the story. What clues foreshadow each event? Complete the chart.

Foreshadowing

An author uses **foreshadowing** to give clues about events that will happen later in the story. For example, if the author says a character cannot swim, that character may later be in danger of drowning.

Saved by a Promise

"Must you go today, Abuelita?" Marta asked Gramma Isela. "A winter storm can come up so quickly in the forest."

"Belen's family needs the food and blankets. I promised her I would go today and she knows I always keep my promises. Don't worry. Turi will be my eyes," said Gramma Isela as her hawk landed on her arm.

When the blizzard hit just a few hours later, Gramma Isela was far from shelter. Her feet could no longer find the path in the falling snow. Then Turi squawked, tugged on Gramma's arm, and led her to a small cave. Isela sank to her knees and whispered to Turi, "Thank you. Now, go find help, my clever friend." Turi squawked happily and flew off into the wind.

After a while Gramma Isela heard voices outside the cave. Belen and her son were calling her name.

"You saved me," said Gramma Isela.

"Your promise and Turi saved you," replied Belen. "You said you would come today, so we started looking for you as soon as it started to snow. Then Turi led us to you. Come to our cabin now and rest."

Event	Foreshadowing Clue
Belen and her son look for Gramma Isela because they know she keeps her promises.	The title of the story is
Gramma Isela gets lost in a storm.	
Turi finds a cave to protect Gramma Isela from the storm.	
Turi brings Belen to help.	

Predict the Outcome

DIRECTIONS Work with a partner. Follow the steps to predict an outcome for "The Lady, or the Tiger?"

1 Review the details in the prediction charts you made as you read the story.

2 Use these details to help you complete the chart below. Write what the information shows about the princess.

3 Make a prediction. Tell which door you think the princess chose and why.

Details and Information	What the Information Shows	Prediction
The princess loved the young man.	The princess would want the young man to be happy.	
She knew what was behind each door.		

DIRECTIONS Use your prediction to write an ending for the story. Tell how the princess felt before she made her decision and what she decided to do. Tell how the crowd reacted to the young man's fate. Use verbs in the past perfect tense.

_____

_____

_____

_____

Where's the Action?

DIRECTIONS Complete the map for "The Lady, or the Tiger?" For the resolution, use the story ending you and your partner wrote.

Story Structure

Most stories have several parts.

- The **conflict** is the story problem.
- During the **rising action**, events lead to a climax. **Complications** are events that make the problem more difficult; the **climax** is the turning point when you learn about the outcome.
- During the **falling action**, events lead to a resolution. The **resolution** answers the remaining questions about the story.

Map of Rising and Falling Action

Characters: _____

Setting: _____

Climax: _____

_____

Complication:

_____

_____

FALLING ACTION

Complication:

_____

_____

RISING ACTION

Resolution: _____

Complication:

_____

_____

_____

Conflict: _____

_____

The Lady, or the Tiger?
LEVEL C TE page T233

105

Unit 4 | Choices

Create a Bibliography

DIRECTIONS Study the entry for a bibliography.
Then complete the sentences.

Citing Sources

When you use the work of others in a report, you must **cite**, or show, your sources. A **bibliography** is an alphabetical list of sources.

author ———— article title ———— page numbers

McCloud, Anna. "Arenas Through the Ages,"
magazine title —— *Junior Archaeologist*, December, 2002, 56–61.
———— publication date

book title ———— Nardo, Don. *The Roman Colosseum.* San Diego: ———— city of publication

publisher ———— Lucent Books. 1998.
copyright date ———— copyright date

Tillery, Kristopher A. (1998–1999). "What is the ————
Colosseum?" page 3. Retrieved 4-15-00 from the
page number —— World Wide Web: http://www.aislagos.com/senate/ ———— article title
when downloaded
and printed dat.uasupport/dat.navigation/dat.architecture/ ———— Web site address

1. When citing a source, the first thing you write is _____ .

2. Article titles are punctuated with _____ .

3. For each source, the only line <u>not</u> indented is the _____ .

4. When citing an Internet source, the last thing listed is _____ .

DIRECTIONS Create a bibliography. Rewrite the information for each source in the correct order. List the sources alphabetically.

Ancient Wonders of the World. Philadelphia:
Bayside Press. Southers, Cynthia. 1999.

Boston: 2001. Phillips, Roy. *Ancient
Buildings.* Miller Books.

April, 40–44. 1998, "Stadiums and Arenas,"
Jones, Roger. *Architecture Today,*

_____

_____

_____

_____

_____

_____

© Hampton-Brown

The Lady, or the Tiger?
LEVEL C TE page T234

106

Unit 4 | Choices

Compare Cultures Through Architecture

DIRECTIONS Follow the steps to compare ancient and modern arenas or stadiums.

1 Research and take notes about arenas.

2 Choose one ancient and one modern arena. Sketch them or use photos. Label parts and architectural features.

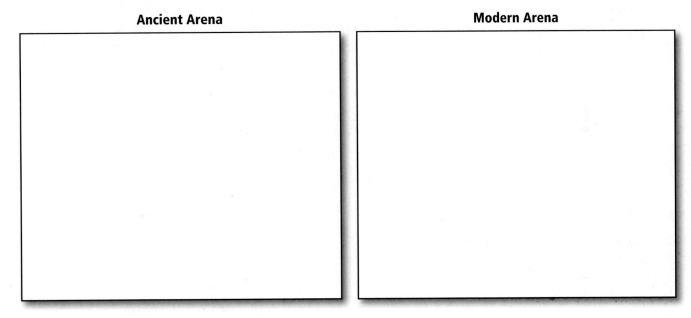

Ancient Arena   **Modern Arena**

3 Complete the chart to compare the arenas.

	Ancient Arena	Modern Arena
Name		
Location		
Size (capacity)		
Architecture (style, color, material)		
Uses		

4 Present the chart as part of a report to the class.

CONTENT AREA CONNECTIONS

Present a Play

DIRECTIONS Work in a group. Brainstorm possibilities as you follow the steps to write and perform a one-act play of "The Lady, or the Tiger?" Be creative. If you like, you may change the setting and add interesting new characters and scenes.

1. Tell where and when the story takes place. Brainstorm **settings**. Then choose and describe one.

   Setting: _____

   _____

   _____

   _____

   _____

2. Give names to the main characters from the story and tell what they are like. Brainstorm other **characters** you want to add.

   Characters: _____

   _____

   _____

   _____

   _____

   _____

   _____

3. What will happen? Will you add any new events? Will you reveal any secrets? Summarize the **plot** of your play.

   Plot: _____

   _____

   _____

   _____

   _____

   _____

   _____

   _____

   _____

   _____

The Lady, or the Tiger?
LEVEL C TE page T234

108

Unit 4 | Choices

4. Write the **theme.** Tell what you want the audience to learn.

Theme: _____

_____

_____

5. Decide how many **scenes** this play will have. Number each scene and give the time and place.

Title: _____

Scene 1: _____

_____

_____

_____

_____

_____

_____

_____

_____

6. Think about each scene. Describe the **set** (scenery) and list any **props** you will need.

Set and Props: _____

_____

_____

_____

_____

_____

7. Choose a **job** for each group member. Check the box for your job.

Jobs:
☐ Scriptwriters: Use the format shown on page 67 for "User Friendly." Write dialogue and stage directions. Include lines for a narrator if neeeded.

☐ Actors: Memorize your lines and movements.

☐ Directors: Help the actors decide how to say their lines and move.

☐ Set Designers: Make the stage look the way you and the directors want it.

☐ Technical Crew: Move props; do the lighting; create sound effects.

☐ Publicity: Tell people about the play. Help them get seated.

The Lady, or the Tiger?
LEVEL C TE page T234

109

Unit 4 | Choices

Say It Another Way

DIRECTIONS Copy lines from each stanza of "The Road Not Taken." Draw or describe the picture they make in your mind. Then paraphrase the lines.

Visualize and Paraphrase

When you **paraphrase** a sentence or paragraph, you **visualize** in your mind what it means. Then you restate it in your own words.

Original sentence: A vast blanket of ice and snow stretched before their eyes.

Paraphrase: All they could see was ice and snow.

Picture:

Stanza 1: Two roads diverged in a yellow wood, And sorry I could not travel both

Paraphrase: A road in a forest split in two and went in different directions. I wished I could see where both parts of the road went.

Picture:

Stanza 2: _____

Paraphrase: _____

Picture:

Stanza 3: _____

Paraphrase: _____

Picture:

Stanza 4: _____

Paraphrase: _____

© Hampton-Brown

LEARN KEY VOCABULARY

Words About Special Athletes

Locate and Use Definitions

DIRECTIONS Guess the meaning of each new word. Then write the Glossary definition. Make a check if your guess is correct.

Term	Guess	Definition	✓
able–bodied person	someone who isn't sick	someone with a strong, healthy body	✓
capable			
coach			
dash			
deuce			
disabled athlete			
double below–the–knee amputee			
event			
personal best			
prosthesis			
single–leg amputee record			
test of will			
track meet			

What Makes Aimee Run?

DIRECTIONS Think about Aimee's career as a fashion model and public speaker. List character traits and motives that make her a success.

Character Traits and Motives

The qualities of someone's personality are called **character traits**.

He was **cheerful, hard working**, and **generous**.

The reasons for a person's actions are called **motives**.

Her **desires for fame and personal satisfaction** drove her to excel as an athlete.

Aimee's Character Traits

1. She is courageous. _____

2. _____

3. _____

4. _____

Aimee's Motives

5. She likes to see how much she can do. She says, "there are so many things I want to explore."

6. _____
_____

7. _____
_____

8. _____
_____

Aimee Mullins is a fashion model.

DIRECTIONS Think about a career you might choose. How will your character traits and motives help you succeed? Complete the chart.

Career: _____

My Traits and Motives	How They Will Help Me Succeed

SUM IT UP

Sequence Information and Monitor Your Reading

DIRECTIONS What important choices did Aimee and her parents make. Complete the time line. Use the Point-by-Point feature in your book for ideas.

Aimee's Choices

Aimee decided

Aimee's parents chose to have her legs amputated.

DIRECTIONS Write a paragraph about monitoring your reading. Review the strategies on page 238 of your book. Then answer the questions:

• How did monitoring your reading help you create the time line?

• Which strategy helped you understand the most?

• How will you use monitoring strategies when you read a new selection?

_____

_____

_____

_____

_____

_____

_____

Root for Yourself!

DIRECTIONS Work with a partner. Use the meanings of Greek and Latin roots to expand your English vocabulary.

1 **Complete the Chart** Write as many words as you can that contain the Greek or Latin root. Check each word in a dictionary. Does it really come from the root?

Greek and Latin Roots

Recognizing **Greek and Latin roots** can help you understand the meanings of new words.

Root	Meaning	English Words
cycl	circle, ring	bicycle
ped	foot	pedestrian

Greek and Latin Roots

Root	Meaning	English Words
aud	hear	audience, audition, auditorium, audiovisual, audible, auditory
fer	carry	
graph	write	
loc	place	
path	feel, suffer	
phon	sound	
spir	breathe	

© Hampton-Brown

2 **Study the Chart** Learn some new roots.

More Greek and Latin Roots

Root	Meaning	English Word
act	do	actor
ast	star	astronaut
bio	life	biosphere
dic	speak	predict
meter	measure	thermometer
mob	move	mobile
photo	light	photography
scop	see	microscope
therm	heat	thermos
voc	voice	advocate

As an athlete, Aimee mobilizes all her resources to do her very best in every event.

3 **Complete the Sentences** Use a word that contains the root in parentheses. Make sure your words fit the context of the sentence by checking their definitions in a dictionary.

1. We read a short _____biography_____ of Aimee Mullins. (**bio**)

2. It included several _____ of her. (**graph**)

3. Before I read the biography, I did not realize that _____ is harder for amputees than for others. (**spir**)

4. I also learned that Aimee's prosthetic legs give her a lot of _____. (**mob**)

5. She can run and skate and do most _____ that others do. (**act**)

6. When she speaks to an _____ full of people, she is personal and provocative. (**aud**)

7. Aimee has _____ for others. (**path**)

8. She is an _____ for others with disabilities. (**voc**)

9. What an amazing amount of _____ she must have! (**spir**)

10. If I met Aimee Mullins, I would definitely ask for her _____. (**graph**)

© Hampton-Brown

It's Our Intention

By the time the flood water is gone, farmers in this community will have suffered many losses.

> ### Future Perfect Tense
> The **future perfect tense** tells about an action that will be completed at a specific time in the future. At least that is the intention. It uses the helping verbs **will have** followed by the **past participle** of the main verb.
>
> By five o'clock, volunteers **will have sandbagged** the river.

DIRECTIONS Complete each sentence. Use the future perfect tense of the verb in parentheses. See Handbook pages 450-451 for a list of irregular past participles.

1. By this time tomorrow, the Placer River ___will have risen___ above flood stage. (**rise**)

2. Authorities _____ emergency procedures. (**begin**)

3. They _____ residents in nearby towns. (**evacuate**)

4. By the time the rain stops, the damage _____ billions of dollars. (**reach**)

5. Many residents _____ their homes swamped by flood water. (**see**)

6. Acres of agricultural land _____ under water. (**disappear**)

7. Bridges _____ . (**collapse**)

8. Some people _____ . (**die**)

9. Rescue workers _____ their lives to save people and animals. (**risk**)

10. Many people _____ their gratitude to rescue workers. (**express**)

MORE ABOUT THE FUTURE PERFECT TENSE Look at the photograph. What might have happened by the end of the next day, by the end of the next week, or by the end of the next month? Write sentences using the future perfect tense.

Words About World War II

New Words

diplomat

Holocaust

issue

Jew

Nazi soldier

official written permission

refugee

survivor

visa

Relate Words

DIRECTIONS Tell more about the word in the center of each box. Use the new words.

```
visa


issued by an embassy
```

```



Holocaust


```

Use New Words in Context

DIRECTIONS Use the new words in sentences. Give more details about each box.

1. _____

   _____

2. _____

   _____

LITERARY ANALYSIS: SETTING

A Time and Place for Everything

DIRECTIONS Read the story. Underline the words and phrases that describe the setting. Then answer the questions.

Rosie the Riveter

When the United States entered World War II, people hated Nazism and wanted to defeat Hitler. Many men and women went off to fight in Europe. Most women like me stayed at home managing the households.

The Allies needed factories to build equipment for the war. There were many factories here in the United States, but there were not enough men to work in them. This gave me a new choice. I asked myself, "How can I best support the war effort?"

In 1945 I joined 19 million other American women who chose to work in the factories. Partly because of this important workforce, the Allies were successful in halting the spread of Nazism in Europe. People used the name "Rosie the Riveter" to honor us for our role in the victory. I am proud that I was a part of that!

American women work on an airplane.

1. When and where does the story take place? _____

2. How does the setting affect the events in the story? Factories needed workers because _____

_____ .

3. How does the setting affect the actions of the characters? The narrator _____

DIRECTIONS Read about a new setting for a similar story. Then answer the questions.

New Setting

It is the year 2020. Rosie lives with her children on Earth. A new space station for adults only has been built in an orbit around Mars. The universal government offers to pay adults to move there and help with important reasearch.

4. When and where will the story take place?

_____

5. How will the setting affect the events of the

story? The government will _____ .

6. How will the setting affect the actions of the characters? Rosie must choose

_____ .

Our Week in Japan

DIRECTIONS You are planning a trip to Japan. Complete each sentence to tell what you intend to see or do. Use the future perfect tense of the verbs in the box. See Handbook pages 450–451 for a list of irregular past participles.

Future Perfect Tense
The **future perfect tense** tells about an action that will be completed at a specific time in the future. It uses the helping verbs **will have** or **shall have** followed by a <u>past participle</u> of a main verb.

By noon, **we will have arrived** in Tokyo.

learn	see	sleep	eat
listen	buy	ride	tell
speak	watch	visit	take
climb	meet	discuss	plan

1. By the time we arrive in Japan, we <u>will have planned</u> _____

<u>our trip for months</u> _____ .

2. By the end of our first day, we _____

_____ .

3. By the end of the next day, we _____

_____ .

4. By the middle of the week, we _____

_____ .

5. By Thursday, we _____

_____ .

6. By Friday afternoon, we _____

_____ .

7. By the end of our stay, we _____

_____ .

8. By this time next year, we _____

_____ .

Kabuki performer

bullet train

sumo wrestlers

Buddhist temple

A Solution for Every Problem

DIRECTIONS Read the story. Then complete the problem-and-solution chart.

The New Cousin

Pierre had always loved his home. He lived on a farm near the French city of Vichy. Even when Hitler invaded France, Pierre felt sure he could protect and feed his family if he did not offend the Nazis.

Then one day in 1940 Pierre faced a difficult choice. A teen-aged Jewish boy named Yacob, starved nearly to death, stumbled out of the forest near Pierre's farm.

Pierre's heart went out to Yacob, but he was afraid to take him in.

Pierre discussed the situation with his wife. "We have never failed to help someone in need before," Anna replied. "We will say that Yacob is our nephew who has come to help us on the farm."

"Ah," sighed Pierre, "I can always count on you to see the obvious." Then he called his children to come meet their new cousin.

Problem:

On the Surface:

Under the Surface:

Solution:

DIRECTIONS Use your chart to write a summary paragraph about the story.

State the problem in your topic sentence. _____

Turn your details into sentences that tell more about Pierre's problem. _____

Explain the solution in your concluding sentence. _____

· GRAMMAR: CONDITIONAL SENTENCES

If People Help . . .

DIRECTIONS Read each sentence and look at the underlined verb. Then complete the sentence using the correct form of the verb in parentheses. Use *would, could, can, will,* or *might* as part of the verb.

> **Conditional Sentences**
>
> **Conditional sentences** tell how one thing depends upon another. They often use helping verbs like **would, could, can, will,** and **might.** Words like **if, unless,** and **as long as** set up the condition in one clause.
>
> If more people acted like Sugihara, the world **might be** better.
>
> If **had** is used in the clause that sets up the condition, use **have** in the other clause.
>
> If I **had been** there, I **would have helped**.

1. If Sugihara <u>had been</u> selfish, he _____would_____

   ___have refused___ to help the people. (**refuse**)

2. Unless he <u>helped</u> the refugees, he

   _____ terrible. (**feel**)

3. Unless the Polish refugees <u>got</u> visas, the Nazis

   _____ them. (**imprison**)

4. If Sugihara <u>had obeyed</u> his government, thousands of people

   _____ . (**die**)

5. If they <u>could enter</u> Japan, they _____ on
   to another country. (**go**)

6. As long as there <u>was</u> time, Sugihara _____
   visas. (**write**)

7. As long as he <u>prepared</u> the visas, the refugees

   _____ hopeful. (**be**)

8. If Sugihara's wife <u>had</u> not <u>encouraged</u> him, he

   _____ writing. (**stop**)

9. If Sugihara <u>had</u> not <u>been</u> sent to Berlin, he

   _____ more people. (**help**)

10. When people <u>overcome</u> their fears, they

    _____ courageous acts. (**perform**)

If you want to travel to another country, you need a visa.

LITERARY ANALYSIS: POINT OF VIEW

Who Tells the Story?

DIRECTIONS Follow these steps to rewrite a scene from "Passage to Freedom."

1 **Choose a character. Who will you be?**

☐ a Jewish refugee at the gate

☐ one of the refugees invited in to talk

☐ another member of the Sugihara family

2 **Choose a scene from the story to rewrite from your character's point of view.**

Scene: _____

3 **List details that answer these questions:**

• What does your character remember about the events of this scene?

_____

• What does your character see and hear? _____

• What does your character hope for? _____

• How does your character feel about the events? _____

4 **Write your character's story. Then share it with your group. Compare points of view.**

_____'s Story

_____

_____

_____

_____

_____

_____

_____

_____

> ### Character's Point of View
> When a story is told from a **character's point of view**, the action is described as a person involved in the story sees it. The narrator expresses that character's personal feelings, thoughts, and memories.
>
> "Passage to Freedom" is told from the point of view of the character, Hiroki Sugihara.

© Hampton-Brown

Atlas and Map Skills

DIRECTIONS Answer the questions about using an atlas.

> **Atlas**
>
> An **atlas** is a collection of maps. Atlases may contain information about climate, population, industry, historical events and other topics. Some atlases are books. Electronic atlases include a **CD-ROM atlas** and an **on-line atlas**.

Some Types of Maps in an Atlas

Political maps show borders, capitals, and major cities.

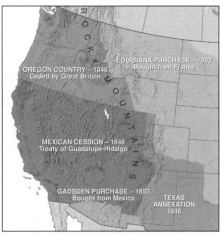

Historical maps show when and where certain events happened.

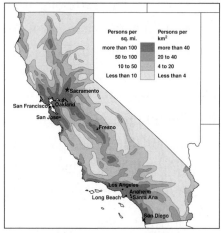

Other maps show a variety of information. This one shows population density.

1. What are the benefits of using an atlas? _____

   _____

2. An atlas may contain maps that show special information. What kinds of information

   do these maps provide? _____

   _____

3. The borders of many countries change over time. What kind of map would show the

   borders that existed in an area many years ago? _____

DIRECTIONS Find maps of one country in an atlas. Answer the questions.

4. What country did you look up? What continent is it on or closest to? _____

   _____

5. Does the country have a natural border, such as a river, ocean, or mountain range?

   Name the natural feature(s). _____

6. What countries border this country? _____

Explore Geography

DIRECTIONS Make a map of Europe. Show the area occupied by the Axis
countries during the early part of World War II. (The Axis countries were
Germany and those that fought on its side.)

1 **Use various sources to find maps:**

- Try history textbooks or library books.

- Use a historical atlas of World War II.

- Look in encyclopedias and almanacs.

- Search the Internet. One key phrase you can use is "maps Europe World War II."
  Brainstorm other key words.

2 **Complete the historical map of Europe.**

- Draw the borders that existed at that time. Label countries.

- Use shading, stripes, or color to show occupied areas.

- Draw a legend that explains your map symbols.

Title and Date: _____

Legend

Words About Decisions

New Words

- alternative
- consider
- decision
- endanger
- option
- reason
- regret
- risk
- setback

Use Context Clues

DIRECTIONS Read each sentence. Then write the new word that completes it.

1. _____ I learned that telling a secret can ____ a friendship.

2. _____ I knew I should ____ the possible results before I spoke.

3. _____ I was aware of the ____ but told his secret anyway.

4. _____ Seeing his face, I began to ____ telling his secret.

5. _____ After thinking long and hard, I reached a ____ .

6. _____ I would have to apologize. There was no ____ .

7. _____ I tried to ____ with my friend, but he wouldn't listen.

8. _____ Telling his secret caused a big ____ in our friendship.

9. _____ The only ____ left was to keep trying to explain.

Use New Words in Context

DIRECTIONS Choose two new words that go together, and write them in the same sentence. Use all the new words. Get ideas from pages 265–267.

10. _____

_____

11. _____

_____

12. _____

_____

13. _____

_____

14. _____

_____

How Do They Relate?

DIRECTIONS Work with a partner. Discuss the chart.
Talk about how each pair of ideas is related.

Analogies

An **analogy** is a comparison based on how two
ideas relate to each other. Each part of this
analogy has a synonym pair.

Synonym Pairs

Small is to little   as   big is to large.

Analogies can be shown in different ways.

Analogy	How the Ideas Are Related
Breakfast is to lunch as bud is to flower.	sequence
Tired is to sleep as hungry is to eat.	cause and effect
Bear is to den as bee is to hive.	place
2 is to 6 as 5 is to 15.	number values
finger : hand : : page : book	part and whole
canvas : painter : : camera : photographer	tool and who uses it
pencil : write : : fork : eat	object and how it is used
post office : mail : : school : desks	object and what it contains

DIRECTIONS Work with a partner. Read each analogy. Discuss how
the pairs of ideas are related. Then complete the analogy.

1. Bird is to sky as fish is to _____sea_____ .

2. Rain is to wet as _____ is to dry.

3. Toe is to foot as _____ is to the U.S.

4. 1/2 is to 1 as 50% is to _____ .

5. Seed is to sprout as _____ is to chick.

6. Glass is to break as paper is to _____ .

7. Tidy is to neat as filthy is to _____ .

8. dictionary : definitions : : atlas : _____ .

9. win : lose : : _____ : front.

10. one : three : : single : _____ .

LITERARY ANALYSIS: ALLUSION

All About Allusions

DIRECTIONS Work with a partner. Use pages 265-267 and "Melba's Choice" to complete the chart.

Allusions

Sometimes a writer refers to a well-known person, place, or event to symbolize an idea or concept. This is called an **allusion**.

The first astronauts on the moon were the **Lewis and Clark** of lunar exploration.

Symbol	What the Symbol Means
Rosa Parks	
The March on Washington	
Little Rock, Arkansas	

DIRECTIONS Read the passage. Then explain what each allusion means in the passage.

Civil Rights Heroes

In the spirit of Rosa Parks, many people around the world are peacefully fighting for civil rights even today. Not every incident is a March on Washington, but each action is important.

The news media may not cover every Little Rock, but the battles in small towns and large cities everywhere are essential to the global struggle for civil rights.

1. _____

_____

2. _____

_____

3. _____

_____

4. Discuss with your partner how your knowledge about the allusions helped you understand.

GRAMMAR: PARTICIPIAL PHRASES

Fighting for a Cause

DIRECTIONS Combine each pair of sentences using a participial phrase. Underline the noun or nouns described by the phrase.

Melba Pattillo
in 1957

> **Participial Phrases**
>
> A **participial phrase** describes a noun. It begins with a **participle**. Most participles end in **–ed** or **–ing**.
>
> **Stunned by shouts of protest,** Elizabeth stood still.
>
> A participial phrase must be placed next to the noun it describes.
>
> **Walking down the street,** Melba saw Central High.
> *Not:* Melba saw Central High **walking down the street.**

1. The street was full of people. They were pushing against one another.

   The street was full of <u>people</u> pushing against one another.

   _____

2. People gazed toward the center of the turmoil. They craned their necks.

   _____

   _____

3. Elizabeth was standing in front of the high school. Melba saw her.

   _____

   _____

4. Melba was surrounded by shouting protesters. She tried to slip away.

   _____

   _____

5. A man chased Melba and her mother. He enlisted others to join him.

   _____

   _____

6. Melba and her mother ran. They were scared by the angry crowds.

   _____

   _____

© Hampton-Brown

SUM IT UP

Analyze a Decision

DIRECTIONS Read the story. Complete the decision matrix.

Connie's Choice

"It's not your fault," my friends say. "You'll just make a bunch of enemies."

I know they're right. If I tell about the cheating and the other kids find out, my teammates will never forget it.

Another little voice says something quite different. "If you don't tell, you could endanger your grade. You might get a zero on your project. You could even fail the class!"

The cheaters, you see, are me and my science project teammates. Gina found the diagrams from a project that got an "A" last year. Everyone else on my team agreed we should do the same project. They said that we would be sure to get a good grade.

Mr. Salazar had told us that our projects must be original. A project that was copied would earn a zero. Worse yet, Mr. Salazar would never trust me again if he found out.

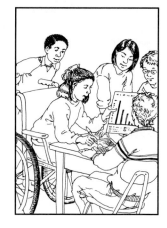

"My conscience is clear," I tell myself. "I argued and argued against the idea but they all said I'd be sorry if I didn't go along with the team vote. I gave in but never agreed." Now it's too late. Mr. Salazar is grading the projects tonight. Shall I report the cheating or just let it go and see what happens?

When I get home, I stop cold in front of the hall mirror. The person staring out at me is the one I have to face every day. Before I even drop my book bag, I find my fingers dialing Mr. Salazar's number.

Decision Matrix

CHOICE:	
PRO:	**CON:**
DECISION:	
What I would have done:	

Past, Present, or Future?

"…in spite of the difficulties and frustrations of the moment, I still have a dream…I have a dream that my four little children will one day live in a nation where they will not be judged by the color of their skin but by the content of their character."

—Martin Luther King, Jr.
from his speech,
"I Have a Dream"

Perfect Tenses

The **present perfect tense** tells about an action that began in the past and may still be going on.

> The topic **has inspired** me.
> I **have gained** admiration for Melba.

The **past perfect tense** tells about an action completed before another action in the past.

> I **had done** research before I went to class.

The **future perfect tense** tells about an action that will be completed at a specific time in the future.

> By tomorrow, I **will have finished** my report.

DIRECTIONS Read each sentence. Underline each verb that is in a perfect tense. Then write *present perfect*, *past perfect*, or *future perfect* to identify the tense.

1. Many people <u>have read</u> about the Civil Rights Movement.

   _____present perfect_____

2. By the time students finish Melba's story, they will have learned a lot.

   _____

3. Schools have changed greatly since the 1950s.

   _____

4. By the end of this decade, many more changes will have occurred.

   _____

5. Before Martin Luther King, Jr. gave his "I Have a Dream" speech, school integration had begun.

   _____

6. Melba had attended Horace Mann before she went to Central High.

   _____

7. She had agreed to go to Central High before she told her parents.

   _____

8. Melba's family has remained in Little Rock.

   _____

9. The struggle for civil rights has inspired people.

   _____

10. Hopefully, before the end of the twenty-first century, we will have met the goals of the Civil Rights Movement.

    _____

MORE ABOUT PERFECT TENSES Write a letter from Melba to Martin Luther King, Jr. Give yourself one point for each perfect tense verb you use. Give yourself another point if you correctly identify the tense. Six points or more is a winning letter!

Deliver a Newscast

DIRECTIONS Pretend you are a TV news reporter. Choose an episode, or event, from "Melba's Choice." Write facts in the chart. Include details about both Melba's experience and the experiences of others.

Newscast

A **newscast** is a radio or television program that reports facts about an event. It answers the questions *Who? What? Where? When?* and *Why?* A newscast includes accurate and complete information. It does not include opinions.

Episode:	
Who? List the people involved.	
What? List the major actions.	
Where? Name the location.	
When? Give dates and times.	
Why? List causes of the event. Avoid stating opinions.	

DIRECTIONS Listen to a real newscast. Then use the information in your chart to write an imaginary newscast. Deliver your newscast to your class.

Report what happened. Include details about how people acted, but do not express your personal opinions about the event.

_____

_____

_____

_____

_____

At the end of your report, give your name and the name of your imaginary news service.

_____

_____

_____

© Hampton-Brown

You Be the Critic

DIRECTIONS Watch a television newscast and use the left side of the chart to evaluate it. Then give your newscast about "Melba's Choice." Ask a classmate to evaluate your report.

TV Newscast	My Newscast
Reporter: _____	Name: _____
TV show: _____	Evaluator: _____
Topic: _____	Topic: _____
Put a check next to the things that are done well.	**Put a check next to the things that are done well.**
The 5Ws are answered . . . . ☐	The 5Ws are answered . . . . ☐
Both sides of the story are told . . . . ☐	Both sides of the story are told . . . . ☐
The information is complete . . . . ☐	The information is complete . . . . ☐
Enough details are given . . . . ☐	Enough details are given . . . . ☐
Opinions are not expressed . . . . ☐	Opinions are not expressed . . . . ☐
The reporter speaks clearly . . . . ☐	The reporter speaks clearly . . . . ☐
Suggestions for improvement:	**Suggestions for improvement:**
_____	_____
_____	_____
_____	_____
_____	_____
_____	_____
_____	_____
_____	_____

Using Periodicals

DIRECTIONS Read each paragraph. Write the type of periodical it describes.

1. *California Medicine* is published by the California Medical Group, an organization of doctors and other medical professionals. It contains reports about medical research. It is published four times a year.

_____

2. The *Ayer Herald* is published daily. It has articles about world and local news. It has several sections, such as Business and Entertainment.

_____

3. *Sports Monthly* has news about all the major sports. It features articles about athletes and teams. It also contains colorful photos of the action.

_____

Periodicals

A **periodical** covers a specific **period** of time. It is published on a regular schedule, such as daily, weekly, or monthly. The most common periodicals are:

- **Newspapers** that contain news reports.

- **Magazines** that contain news, other articles, and photos. They may also feature specific subjects, such as cars or music.

- **Journals** for professional organizations contain articles about topics related to the organizations.

DIRECTIONS Study the sample. Then answer the questions.

Sample from the
*Readers' Guide to
Periodical Literature*

CIVIL rights
   Civil rights; address, December 29, 1960.
      W. P. Rogers. Vital speeches 27:218-20
      Ja 15 '61
   Civil rights code offered. Sr Schol 74:37 F 20
      '59
   Civil rights deadlock. New Repub 142:2 Ja
      25 '60
   Civil rights legislation. New Repub 140:4-5
      Mr 30 '59
   Civil rights planks. Commonweal 72:365 Jl 22
      '60

4. Which is the most recent article? _____

5. Which periodical has an article about a speech? _____

6. Which two articles are about civil rights laws? Write the titles.

_____

_____

Evaluate Sources of Information

DIRECTIONS With a group, analyze two newspaper or two magazine articles about a specific event during the Civil Rights Movement. Complete the chart to compare them.

Event and Date: _____

	Article 1	Article 2
Title		
Author		
Source		
Author's Beliefs or Opinions What does the author say that tells what he or she thinks is true?		
Author's Judgments What opinions does the author form after careful study and comparison?		
Author's Bias or Prejudice Does the author favor one side more than the other without enough reason? Explain.		

Content Summary: How is the information in one article different from the other?

_____

_____

_____

_____

UNIT 5 MIND MAP

Triumphs

DIRECTIONS Use the mind map to show how you can break through barriers and triumph. As you read the selections in this unit, add new ideas you learn about triumphs.

Triumphs

Breaking Through

Barriers

Tell Me More

DIRECTIONS Write compound, complex, and compound-complex sentences by combining each set of sentences into one. Use conjunctions and relative pronouns from the word bank.

> **Example:**
> Times were bad. People struggled to survive.
> Times were bad, but people struggled to survive.
>   **or**
> Although times were bad, people struggled to survive.

Sentences with Clauses

An **independent clause** can stand alone as a sentence. A **dependent clause** cannot stand alone because it does not express a complete thought.

Oklahoma had a drought **that** ruined the land.
  independent clause   dependent clause

Clauses can be combined with **conjunctions** and **relative pronouns** to make **compound, complex,** and **compound-complex** sentences.

The rain did not fall, **so** crops died.
Because there was no rain, crops shriveled and died.
The rain stopped, **and** the wind blew up the dry soil **that** covered the land.

1. The fields were ruined. It hadn't rained for years.

   _____

   _____

2. Dust blew over the land. It turned the air red.

   _____

   _____

3. Farmers planted seeds in rows. The rows were deep. The wind blasted the seeds out anyway.

   _____

   _____

4. Farmers planted windbreaks. The trees didn't stop the wind.

   _____

   _____

5. Farm families packed their belongings. They drove to California. They hoped to find work.

   _____

   _____

Word Bank

Coordinating Conjunctions
and   or
but   so
for   yet

Subordinating Conjunctions
although
because
since
when
where

Relative Pronouns
who
whom
whose
that
which

MORE ABOUT CLAUSES Work with a partner. Elaborate by adding adjectives, prepositional phrases, and clauses to your sentences. Write the new sentences.

© Hampton-Brown

Words About Hard Times

New Words

bankruptcy

barren

borrow

collapse

decline

drought

Great
Depression

Panhandle

stock market

unemployment

Locate and Use Definitions

DIRECTIONS Use a dictionary to decide which new words
go together. Then write a sentence to show each relationship.

Words That Go Together:

barren, drought

Sentence: When a drought occurs, there
is no water for the crops, and the land
becomes barren.

_____

Words That Go Together:

_____

Sentence: _____

_____

_____

_____

Words That Go Together:

_____

Sentence: _____

_____

_____

_____

Words That Go Together:

_____

Sentence: _____

_____

_____

_____

Words That Go Together:

_____

Sentence: _____

_____

_____

_____

© Hampton-Brown

Get Personal!

DIRECTIONS Read the passage. Underline each example of personification. Then complete the chart.

> Just getting from the barn to the house seemed to take an eternity. The wind was <u>determined</u> to keep me from making any progress. Digging deep into the topsoil, he tossed handfuls of gray dust into my eyes. His cruel fingers grabbed my coat and clawed every inch of exposed flesh. Screaming and moaning his rage, he kicked my boots out from under me, chuckling at my fall with evil laughter.

Personification

Personification is giving human characteristics to things that are not human. The writer might say a thing has human **motives**, **sounds**, **actions**, or even **physical traits**.

The rain's cool **hand bathed** every leaf.

Types of Personification	Examples
Human Motives	determined,
Human Sounds	
Human Actions	
Human Physical Traits	

DIRECTIONS Write a paragraph about the Dust Bowl. Give human characteristics to the wind, dust, or land. Have a partner identify each example of personification.

A Dusty Time

_____

_____

_____

_____

_____

Dorothea Lange: Photographer

Dorothea Lange, 1936

Dorothea Lange photographed her subjects precisely as she saw them. Her photos help us see what life was like in the Depression.

> ## Compound and Complex Sentences
>
> A **compound sentence** has two or more **independent clauses** joined by a semi-colon or by a comma and a **coordinating conjunction**.
>
> The woman is worried; her children are hungry.
> The woman is worried, **for** her children are hungry.
>
> A **complex sentence** has one **independent clause** and one or more **dependent clauses**. The dependent clause begins with either a **subordinating conjunction** or a **relative pronoun**.
>
> The picture shows a woman **who** lives in a migrant camp.

DIRECTIONS Underline the independent clause or clauses in each sentence. Write *compound* or *complex* to identify the kind of sentence.

Kind of Sentence

1. <u>Dorothea Lange was a photographer</u> who became famous for her realistic pictures of people struggling in tough times.

   complex

2. Lange studied photography in college, but she did not have her first exhibition until years later.

   _____

3. When she was twenty, she decided to travel around the world.

   _____

4. She settled in San Francisco when she ran out of money.

   _____

5. In San Francisco, she opened a portrait studio; she also began concentrating on frank, realistic portrayals of the poor.

   _____

6. In the 1930's, she photographed people whose lives had been affected by the Depression.

   _____

7. She took pictures of homeless men on the streets; she photographed people in breadlines.

   _____

8. The pictures that made her famous were her photographs of migrant workers.

   _____

9. She had great sympathy for the poor and the unemployed people whom she photographed.

   _____

10. Dorothea Lange wanted to show real life, and she succeeded through her photographs.

    _____

LITERARY ANALYSIS: DIALECT

How Do You Say It?

DIRECTIONS Read the different names for each object.
Then write the name you use.

pop
soda
tonic
_____

hoagie
poor boy
sub
_____

bag
tote
sack
_____

flap jacks
hot cakes
pancakes
_____

Dialect

A **dialect** is the way people from a certain area speak. Your dialect includes the ways you pronounce some words and names you use for some objects or events.

Southern U.S.:
"Y'all come along to ma doin's, now."

Canada:
"Come over to my party, eh?"

DIRECTIONS Write sentences that contain dialect from the examples
above. Have your partner rewrite each sentence using a different dialect.

1. Put the hoagie in the sack, please.

   Put the poor boy in the tote, please.

2. _____

   _____

3. _____

   _____

4. _____

   _____

5. _____

   _____

6. _____

   _____

What Is It Like?

DIRECTIONS Read the passage. Underline each simile or metaphor. Then complete the chart.

Figurative Language

Writers use **figurative language** to say things in vivid ways.

A **simile** makes a comparison using *like* or *as*.

   The ranch was **like a cloud of dust.**

A **metaphor** compares by saying that one thing <u>is</u> another thing that has similar qualities.

   The dust **was an endless wall.**

A Farmer's Memories

"My field <u>is an empty, dry desert</u>!" the farmer sighs sadly. She remembers when crops as lush as any jungle had grown in this very soil. The seeds of rice and maize were tiny hopes she had planted. She had cared for each plant like a shepherd tending his sheep. She had filled this field with life. It was her gold mine. Now her dreams have flown away like feathers in the harsh wind.

Metaphors	Similes
is an empty, dry desert	_____
_____	_____
_____	_____
_____	_____
_____	_____

DIRECTIONS Compare a desert and a field. Write a simile and a metaphor. Share your sentences with a partner.

1. _____

_____

2. _____

_____

GRAMMAR: COMPOUND, COMPLEX, AND COMPOUND-COMPLEX SENTENCES

No Escape

DIRECTIONS Work with a partner. Break up the sentences. Write simple sentences.

> **Compound, Complex, and Compound-Complex Sentences**
>
> A **compound sentence** has two or more independent clauses joined by a semi-colon or by a comma and a coordinating conjunction.
>
> > The dust was everywhere; you couldn't hide from it.
>
> A **complex sentence** has one independent clause and one or more dependent clauses.
>
> > It even seeped through windows that had been taped.
>
> A **compound-complex sentence** has two or more independent clauses and one or more dependent clauses.
>
> > You couldn't hide from the dust, for it even seeped through windows and doors that had been taped.

1. In 1931, a drought that started in Oklahoma caused crops to shrivel and die.

   In 1931, a drought started in Oklahoma. It

   caused crops to shrivel and die.

   _____

2. In 1936, farmers suffered even more because dust storms began to roll across their fields.

   _____

   _____

3. People tried to escape the smothering dust, but it was impossible; the dust was everywhere.

   _____

   _____

   _____

4. Storms raced toward the farms, but before they ran for shelter, farmers had to put their animals in the barn.

   _____

   _____

   _____

5. People died in dust storms, or they died from "dust pneumonia," which affected their lungs.

   _____

   _____

   _____

MORE ABOUT COMPOUND, COMPLEX, AND COMPOUND-COMPLEX SENTENCES Identify each sentence above as a simple, compound, complex, or compound-complex sentence. Then write one of each about the Dust Bowl. Have a partner identify the clauses.

© Hampton-Brown

SUM IT UP

Relate Causes and Effects

DIRECTIONS Complete a cause-and-effect chart for each section of "The Dirty Thirties." Then work with a group to write a main idea statement for the entire selection.

Section 1, pages 295–297

What Happened?	Why?
Crops died.	It stopped raining in 1931.

Main Idea:
Because it stopped raining in 1931, many crops died.

Section 3, pages 302–305

What Happened?	Why?

Main Idea:

Section 2, pages 298–301

What Happened?	Why?

Main Idea:

Epilogue, pages 306–307

What Happened?	Why?

Main Idea:

Main Idea of the Selection: _____

_____

_____

GRAMMAR: ADJECTIVES THAT COMPARE

The Hardest Times

A young boy covers his nose against brown sand in the Dust Bowl.

Adjectives That Compare

A **comparative adjective** compares two things.
> Farming was **harder** in the 1930s than in the 1920s.
> Life was **less difficult** in Kansas than in Oklahoma.

A **superlative adjective** compares three or more things.
> The Panhandle was the **hardest** hit region of all.
> The **most difficult** year was 1937.

Use **–er** and **–est** for short adjectives. For long adjectives, use **less / more** and **least / most**.

DIRECTIONS Finish each sentence. Write the correct form of the adjective in parentheses.

1. In the 1930s, people owned small farms; some farms were _____*simpler*_____ than others. (**simple**)

2. The _____ family farms of all had 40 acres or less. (**small**)

3. Once the rains stopped, each year became _____ than the last. (**dry**)

4. Prices for crops were already low, but prices grew _____ every year. (**low**)

5. Of all the people, farmers may be the _____ during a drought. (**vulnerable**)

6. Dry farmers are even _____ during droughts than other farmers. (**defenseless**)

7. Farmers hoped that the next year would be _____ than the last. (**troublesome**).

8. Unfortunately, each dust storm seemed _____ than the last. (**fierce**)

9. On April 14, 1935, the skies grew _____ than ever. (**dark**)

10. It was Black Sunday, and the storm was the _____ dust storm of the year. (**deadly**)

11. In the late 1930s, Oklahoma farmers had to make the _____ decisions of their lives. (**difficult**)

12. Leaving their farms was the _____ decision of all. (**challenging**)

WRITING: A LETTER

Problems and More Problems

DIRECTIONS Write the result of each conflict in "The Dirty Thirties." If the conflict was resolved, explain how.

Type of Conflict	Conflict	Result or Resolution
Person Against Nature	There was no rain for many years. Dry land and wind created the Dust Bowl.	
Person Against Person	Tractor drivers knocked down the bankrupt farmers' houses.	
Person Against Society	California farmers advertised for more workers than they needed.	

DIRECTIONS Pretend you are living in the Oklahoma Panhandle during the 1930s. Write a letter to a friend. Tell about two conflicts you are facing and your plans to resolve them. Use adjectives that compare.

Use an Oklahoma address and a date during the 1930s for the heading.

_____

_____

_____

Include a greeting.   Dear _____ ,

_____

_____

Describe two different types of conflicts and their resolutions.

_____

_____

_____

_____

Your friend,

Include a closing and signature.

_____

The Great Depression

DIRECTIONS Work with a group. Follow the steps to research the effects of the Great Depression in one area of the United States.

Men waiting in line for food during the Great Depression

1 **Brainstorm Areas** Decide what area of the country to research. Select an area like New York City, southern California, or the Midwest.

2 **Narrow Your Topic** Be sure your topic is not too broad. A specific, or smaller, topic is easier to research and to write about. You might research the banking business in New York City, or the film industry in Hollywood, California.

This is a broad topic. | Effects of the Great Depression

The topic has been narrowed to one area. | Effects of the Great Depression in Detroit, Michigan

The topic has been narrowed to a specific industry in one area. | Effects of the Great Depression on the automobile industry in Detroit, Michigan

Our topic: _____

3 **Write Research Questions** Choose the one you will research.

☐ _____

☐ _____

☐ _____

☐ _____

4 **Conduct the Research** Look for answers to your research question in history books, encyclopedias, and on the Internet. Take notes on notecards. Remember to write your sources.

5 **Design a Visual** Review your notes. What information could you show with a chart or diagram? Look at the sample graph below and see the other graphic organizers on Handbook pages 370–373. Then sketch your visual.

Bar Graph

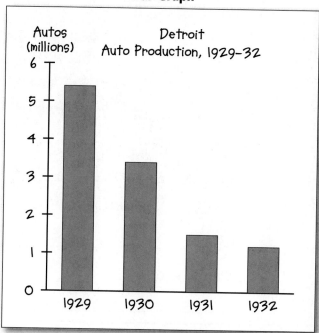

Autos (millions)

Detroit Auto Production, 1929–32

6
5
4
3
2
1
0

1929   1930   1931   1932

Sketch

6 **Write Your Report** Share your notes with your group. Use an outline to organize the group's information. Look at your sketches and decide which visuals to use. See Handbook page 397 for help in making an outline.

• Write, edit, and make a final copy of your report.

• Create the visuals. Use colors and make the visuals large enough for the class to see.

7 **Deliver Your Report** Prepare your report and present it to the class.

• Plan time to present your report.

• Gather any materials you will need to make your presentation, such as a display stand, or video equipment.

• Plan what each member will do during the presentation.

• Present your report to the class. Discuss generalizations about the Great Depression.

RESEARCH SKILLS

Graphic Aids

DIRECTIONS Identify each type of graphic aid. Explain what it shows.

1.

CAUSES AND EFFECTS: 1929-1940

The Stock Market crashes. The Great Depression begins.

Farmers cannot pay their bills. Banks take back control of the farms.

The drought continues. Farmers cannot grow crops.

Without crops, the topsoil dries up. Dust storms blow the dry soil away.

Type: cause-and-effect chart

What it shows: the events that caused the farmers' troubles

2.

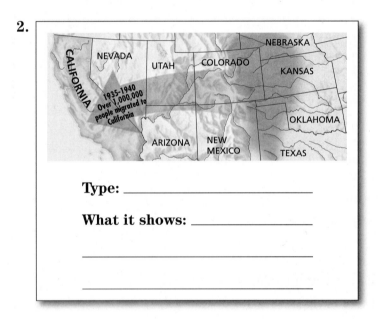

Type: _____

What it shows: _____

_____

_____

3.

| 1929 | | 1931 | 1932 | 1933 | | 1936 |

Stock market crashes; value of crops decreases. — Rain stops; crops die; migration starts. — 1,000 families a week lose farms. — Roosevelt creates New Deal. — The dust storms start.

Type: _____

What it shows: _____

_____

_____

4.

Percent of Unemployment: 1930-1935

(line graph: nationwide, in Kansas; Percent of Unemployment vs Year 1930–1935)

Type: _____

What it shows: _____

_____

_____

5.

Annual Rainfall at Goodwell, Oklahoma: 1931-1940

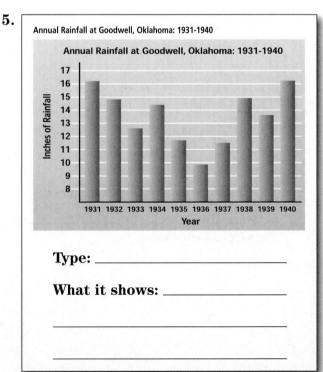

Type: _____

What it shows: _____

_____

_____

© Hampton-Brown

Name _____ Date _____

DIRECTIONS Suppose you are planning a report about southern California during the Great Depression. Tell how you could use graphic aids.

1 See examples of graphic aids on Handbook pages 370–373.
2 Think about the kind of information you could show with each type of graphic aid.
3 Look through reference sources for examples of graphic aids.
4 Write your plan in the chart.

Graphic Aid	Information the Graphic Aid Could Show
Annotated map Source:	
Bar graph Source:	
Cause-and-effect chart Source:	
Line graph Source:	
Time line Source:	

Drought Words

Use New Words in Context

New Words

- comfort
- debt
- diversification
- feud
- flee
- slip
- sorrow
- spindly
- steady
- sustain

DIRECTIONS Complete the paragraph. Use the new words.

Every day we have to _____ feud _____ with the Earth.
                              1.

The winds are _____ and continue to blow. We'd like to
                        2.

_____ away, but we cannot _____
          3.   4.

from the dust. We tried _____ by planting different
                                    5.

vegetables and grains. However, the plants are still _____
                                                                6.

and weak. They can't even _____ a hungry mouse!
                                      7.

How will we pay our _____ to the bank? It fills me
                              8.

with _____ to think about it. At least there is
          9.

_____ in knowing that it will rain some day.
          10.

Relate Words

DIRECTIONS Write eight new words. Then write synonyms for them.

	New Words	Synonyms
11.	_____	_____
12.	_____	_____
13.	_____	_____
14.	_____	_____
15.	_____	_____
16.	_____	_____
17.	_____	_____
18.	_____	_____

Repeating for Emphasis

DIRECTIONS With a partner, take turns reading the poem aloud. Then write each example of repetition and assonance. Underline the repeated sounds for assonance.

> ### Dust Bowl Lament
>
> —Eduardo Feliz
>
> Leaving home
> Wind blows out the past
> No reason to stay.
>
> Leaving home
> Biscuits with mud to eat
> No water flowing.
>
> Leaving home
> Crops just rows of dust
> No life showing.
>
> Leaving home
> Only memories to carry
> No hope of return.

> ### Repetition and Assonance
>
> Sometimes writers repeat sounds, words, and phrases. This is called **repetition**.
>
> "**We'll be back, they say.**
> **We'll be back** when it rains, **they say,**
> Don't forget us, **they say.**"
>
> **Assonance** is the repetition of the same or similar vowel sounds between different consonants.
>
> "...d<u>a</u>mpen the r<u>a</u>gs ."
>
> Writers use repetition and assonance to emphasize ideas and feelings or to create a musical sound.

1. Repetition:

_____

_____

2. Assonance:

_____

_____

A migrant family walks along a highway in Oklahoma. June, 1938.

DIRECTIONS Work with a partner. Write examples of repetition and assonance. Use words from the box and your own words.

main	trick	make	send	stay	take	name	help	pale
tell	rhyme	smile	live	alone	alive	sing	tiny	sip

Repetition	**Assonance**
_____	_____
_____	_____
_____	_____

Repeated Consonants

DIRECTIONS With a partner, take turns reading the poem aloud.
Then write each example of alliteration or consonance.
Underline the repeated sounds.

Alliteration and Consonance

Alliteration is the repetition of consonant sounds at the beginnings of words.

the <u>w</u>inds of

the <u>w</u>ild <u>w</u>est

Consonance is the repetition of consonant sounds in the middle or at the ends of words that have different vowel sounds.

the su<u>n</u> shi<u>n</u>ing <u>in</u>

the la<u>n</u>e

Hard to Explain
—B. J. Owens

It's hard to explain
How empty and dead
Everything feels
So full of dust,
So full, yet so empty.

Such a solid weight
In mouth and eyes
In ears and nose and throat.

Lungs and limbs refuse
To move
In this hard heaviness.

But it's even harder
To explain
Not having the nerve
To leave.

Alliteration:

<u>hard</u>, _____   _____

_____   _____

_____

Consonance:

<u>hard</u>, _____   _____

_____   _____

Billie Jo lived in Oklahoma in the 1930's.

DIRECTIONS Write a short poem using alliteration and consonance. Read it
aloud to a partner. Ask your partner to identify the repeated sounds.

_____   _____

_____   _____

_____   _____

_____   _____

Feelings and Attitudes

DIRECTIONS Read the poem. Then answer the questions.

Mr. Roosevelt's Initials
—F. Tong

I'm not sure who Mr. Roosevelt is,
But he has a lot of initials, like WPA and CCC.
He gave my daddy a job.
First he trained him.
Then he put him to work and paid him.

I don't know what all the initials mean,
But I know that now we eat every day,
And now we have clean water and good clothes,
And Daddy smiles every morning
And squares his shoulders the way Momma does
When she goes to the store with some money in her purse.

> **Mood and Tone**
>
> The **mood** of a selection is how it makes you feel. Words like *happy*, *scared*, and *excited* can describe mood.
>
> The **tone** is how the author expresses his or her attitude about the subject. Words like *angry*, *humorous*, or *caring* can describe tone.

Mood: How does this poem make you feel? _____

Tone:
• What words show the author's feelings? _____

_____

_____

• What do you think the author's attitude is about President Roosevelt's programs? Explain.

The author likes / dislikes President Roosevelt's programs. _____

_____

_____

DIRECTIONS Review each selection and complete the chart.

Selection Title	Mood	Tone
"Listening for a Voice" – page 28		
"Something to Declare" – page 119		
"Brother, Can You Spare a Dime?" – page 292		

Compare Dust Bowl Stories

DIRECTIONS Work with a partner. Read the article. Underline the details that are similar to those in "Out of the Dust." Then complete the comparison chart.

The Migrant Road

The migrants came out of Oklahoma, Texas, Arkansas, and Missouri — a great tide of more than 1 million people that flowed westward through the 1930s in search of work and shelter.

The exodus crossed 180 miles of Texas under the dangling stars of the vast sky; then went 350 miles across New Mexico and on to the Arizona deserts. They journeyed in fragile, faltering cars, some of which died on the road.

Arthur Hayes, a sharecropper in eastern Oklahoma, was among the last to leave for California. Hayes drove a 1929 Model A Ford that "hammered and rattled and smoked."

"You wanted to help them, but you didn't dare," Hayes said. "You couldn't afford to help, so you just left them sitting alongside the road."

The migrant road crawled forward, through the Mojave Desert of California, up past Tehachapi and down the winding grade, and then — a breathtaking stop to stare into the great valley below.

	Out of the Dust	The Migrant Road
Genre	poetry	nonfiction
Author's Purpose		
Writing Style		
Narrator's Point of View		
Mood		
Tone		
Theme		

© Hampton-Brown

Different Descriptions

DIRECTIONS Study each picture. Then use each literary device to describe the scene.

Literary Devices

A **simile** uses *like* or *as* to make a comparison.

Personification gives human qualities or characteristics to animals, objects, or ideas.

Onomatopoeia uses words or phrases that imitate sounds.

1. Similes: _____

_____

2. Personification: _____

_____

3. Onomatopoeia: _____

_____

4. Similes: _____

_____

5. Personification: _____

_____

6. Onomatopoeia: _____

_____

DIRECTIONS Write a paragraph using literary devices to describe one of the scenes. Have a partner identify each example of simile, personification, and onomatopoeia.

_____

_____

_____

_____

_____

CONTENT AREA CONNECTIONS

Have a Debate

DIRECTIONS Work with a group. Follow the steps to plan a debate.

> **Debate**
>
> A **debate** is a discussion between people or groups who disagree about something.

Debate Issue:
Should the government intervene when people need help? Why or why not?

1 **Do Research** Find out about government relief programs during the Great Depression. Use program names in the chart as key words. Complete the chart.

- List the pros, or advantages, of each program. How did it improve people's lives? How did it give them a chance for a better future? How did it help society or nature?

- List the cons, or disadvantages, of each program. Did people become dependent on it? Did it help everyone that needed aid? Were there problems in managing it?

Relief Program	Purpose	Pros	Cons
Old Age Benefits (Social Security)	provide aid for the elderly and others unable to work	provided money to those unable to work; relieved burden on relatives	created a welfare state; may not have enough money in the future
Unemployment Insurance			
Aid to Dependent Children			
Civilian Conservation Corps			

2 **Choose a Position** With your group, discuss the relief programs and choose a position for or against government intervention.

© Hampton-Brown

3 **Support Your Position** Write your arguments and facts from your notes. If you are arguing **for** government intervention, use points from the *Pros* column on page 156. If you are arguing **against**, use points from the *Cons* column.

Our Arguments	Our Supporting Facts

4 **Defend Your Position** Think of arguments the other team might have. Use your notes to write responses, or answers, to their arguments.

Their Arguments	Our Responses and Supporting Facts

5 **Conduct the Debate** Choose group members to present each argument or response. Practice presenting your arguments. Then have a debate with a group that has a different position than yours.

BUILD LANGUAGE AND VOCABULARY

Talk It Over

DIRECTIONS Underline the participial phrase in each sentence. Circle the noun or pronoun it describes.

> ## Participial Phrases
>
> A **participle** is a special verb form. It usually ends in **–ing** or **–ed**. A **participial phrase** begins with a participle. It acts like an adjective to describe a noun or pronoun. A participial phrase must be placed next to the word it describes.
>
> **Overwhelmed by the problem,** Maria asked to see a mediator.
>
> **Not:** Maria asked to see a mediator **overwhelmed by the problem.**

1. Believing the team needed to improve their skills, (Maria) suggested Friday night practices.

2. Angered by Maria's suggestion, Inez said they couldn't do that because she was team captain, and she babysits on Friday nights.

3. Hoping to negotiate a solution, the girls decided to go to peer mediation.

4. The older students sitting in teacher's chairs seemed kind of scary at first.

5. Glancing from the mediators to Inez, Maria began to talk.

6. Trained to be respectful, the mediators listened without interrupting.

7. Wanting to be fair, the mediators asked Inez to share her side of the story.

8. Surprised at the outcome, Inez and Maria were pleased to have practice on Thursdays.

DIRECTIONS Combine each pair of sentences using a participial phrase. Place the phrase before or after the noun it describes. Underline the noun.

9. Coach Gomez was disappointed by his team's lack of effort. He decided to quit.

   Disappointed by his team's lack of effort, Coach Gomez decided to quit.

10. The principal did not want to lose his coach. He asked Coach Gomez to reconsider.

    _____

    _____

11. The team was determined to try harder. They won the next three games.

    _____

    _____

12. Coach Gomez was delighted with their effort. He decided to stay.

    _____

    _____

Words About Maturity

New Words

admit

disappointed

fascinated

mature

miserable

radiant

serious

stupor

widow

Relate Words

DIRECTIONS Look at each word pair. Write a sentence to show how the two words are related.

Word Pairs		Sentences
mature	serious	
disappointed	fascinated	
radiant	stupor	
miserable	widow	

Use New Words in Context

DIRECTIONS Read the paragraph on page 328 of your book. Rewrite it from Grandma's point of view.

_____

_____

_____

_____

_____

_____

Teresita helps her Grandma fix a meal.

_____

_____

_____

_____

How Does It Affect You?

DIRECTIONS Review each selection and complete the chart.
Share your responses with a partner.

Respond to Literature

Your **response to literature** is how you feel about the characters' experiences and the author's message. Your response is based on your experiences, feelings, and opinions.

I understand how he feels . . .

Selection	How is the character's situation like yours?	What does the character learn from the events in the story?	How do the events in the story affect you?
Something to Declare		Appreciate yourself and don't try to be something you are not.	
Aimee Mullins			
Melba's Story			

DIRECTIONS Respond to one of the selections in your book. Include the kinds of details shown in the chart above. Share your paragraph with a partner.

Selection Title: _____

_____

_____

_____

_____

_____

_____

LITERARY ANALYSIS: FLASHBACK

Remember When...

DIRECTIONS Read each story. Then answer the questions.

> **Flashback**
>
> A **flashback** is an interruption in the action of a story to tell about something that happened earlier. Phrases like "he remembered" or "that reminds me," may introduce a flashback.

The Perfect Day

It was a perfect day—almost. Dad and I were making *lumpia* together and sneaking bites of juicy pork and vegetables. Then Dad began criticizing everything I did. Making lumpia wasn't fun anymore. I thought back to when we made lumpia with Mom. We had been so happy then.

Suddenly I realized what was going on. "Dad," I whispered. "I miss Mom too."

Dad sighed. "Thanks for understanding, Dora. Now, how fast can we wrap the rest?"

It was a perfect day after all.

1. What happened in the flashback? _____

_____

2. What words introduced the flashback? _____

3. How does the flashback help you understand Dad's actions? _____

_____

The Broken Reed

It was Elva's turn to try out for the honors orchestra. She warmed up on her oboe. *Squawk*! Her reed broke. She searched through her oboe case but found no reeds.

Then Elva heard Kavi's voice across the room. She remembered last week's rehearsal. Paco had forgotten his music, but Kavi had said, "You can look on with me."

Elva hurried over to where Kavi sat tuning his oboe. "Sure," he replied to her request, "I have an extra reed. Good luck."

Elva just smiled at her new friend.

4. What happened in the flashback? _____

5. What words introduced the flashback? _____

6. How does the flashback help you understand Kavi's actions? _____

_____

SUM IT UP

Evaluate Character Development

DIRECTIONS Follow the steps to evaluate character development.

1 Study the Qualities.

2 Circle a grade for each quality in "The Dance." Then write the overall grade. Use examples from the selection to explain the grades to your group.

Qualities of Character Development
Consider these qualities when you evaluate character development in fiction: • **Descriptions:** Does the author describe characters clearly? • **Dialogue:** Does the dialogue help you understand the characters? • **Actions:** Do the characters' actions seem realistic?

Character Development in "The Dance"

Quality	Grade		
Descriptions	very clear	A B C D F	unclear
Dialogue	very helpful	A B C D F	unhelpful
Actions	very realistic	A B C D F	unrealistic
	Overall Grade: _____		

3 Write an imaginary letter to the author evaluating the character development in "The Dance." Share your letter with your group.

_____

_____

_____

_____

_____

_____

GRAMMAR: PROGRESSIVE FORMS OF VERBS

Things Are Changing

DIRECTIONS Complete each sentence. Use the correct progressive form of the verb. Use the chart to find the right form.

Tense	How to Form the Progressive
Present	Use *am, is,* or *are* + the present participle.
Past	Use *was* or *were* + the present participle.
Future	Use *will be* + the present participle.
Present Perfect	Use *has been* or *have been* + the present participle.
Past Perfect	Use *had been* + the present participle.
Future Perfect	Use *will have been* + the present participle.

Progressive Forms of Verbs

Progressive forms of verbs describe actions that continue over a period of time—in the present, past, or future.

They use a form of the helping verb **be** plus a present participle.

I **am dancing** now.
I **have been dancing** for 11 years.

1. For a long time, Mami ___ has been missing ___ Papi.
   miss; present perfect

2. Yolanda _____ her mother to stay single.
   expect; past perfect

3. Now Don José _____ a lot.
   visit; present perfect

4. He _____ on Mami every night.
   call; present perfect

5. Last night, they _____ at photos when
   Yolanda came home.　　　　　*look; past*

6. Tonight, Mami _____ out with Don José.
   go; present

7. They _____ to the dance.
   go; future

8. Yolanda thinks, "By tomorrow, they _____
   each other for two weeks.　　　*see; future perfect*

9. I _____ that Mami should not date.
   think; present perfect

10. Now I _____ if Papi would just want
    her to be happy."　　*wonder; present*

Ambitious Words

Use Context Clues

New Words

compensation

dignity

dubious

flying machine

noble

petty

pride

pursue

superior

suspicious

DIRECTIONS Write a new word to complete each sentence.

1. Sarita decided to _____ pursue _____ a teaching career.

2. Her sister felt _____ about Sarita's choice.

3. Her mother wanted her to be the pilot of a _____ .

4. Her brother said that flying was a _____ occupation.

5. Even Sarita's friends were _____ about the idea.

6. Sarita felt that teaching was a _____ profession.

7. She admired the _____ of many of her teachers.

8. She knew she could become a _____ teacher.

Use New Words in Context

DIRECTIONS Prepare to act out the scene on page 338 of your book. Write new words to complete what each character will say. Then perform the scene with a partner.

Nephew: Uncle, I have _____ my dream and created my

own _____ .

Uncle: Your machine is a _____ device, but I feel

_____ that it will work. Building that machine

was a _____ way to spend time.

I am _____ that you have wasted your money

and will never get _____ for it.

Nephew: Uncle, I know that you respect my _____ . I also

know that I used a _____ design, so I am sure

the plane will fly. I assure you that your _____

will not suffer because of my dream.

© Hampton-Brown

First, Third, or Third?

DIRECTIONS Read each passage. What pronouns does the narrator use? Whose thoughts, feelings, and experiences does the narrator tell? Identify the point of view and explain how you know.

Narrator's Point of View

In the **first-person** point of view, the narrator is a character in the story and tells only what that character thinks, feels, or experiences.

In the **third-person omniscient**, or all-knowing, point of view, the narrator tells about the thoughts, feelings, and experiences of all the characters.

In the **third-person limited** point of view, the narrator tells only what one character thinks, feels, or experiences.

Quan and Mai Pack

Quan whistled as she packed and wondered about her sister's silence. "What's wrong with Mai?" Quan thought to herself. The move to San Francisco was easy for Quan. She was confident that she could make new friends. But shy Mai was happy in Denver. She had friends and knew her way around. "How can Quan whistle at a time like this?" Mai sighed.

1. Point of view: _____

   Explanation: _____

   _____

   _____

   _____

Mai Dreads Moving

"Mai, hurry up and pack!" called Quan. "The movers are here." Mai had been dreading this moment. She was about to leave her home, her friends, and her school. Her parents wanted to move to San Francisco, but Mai was happy in Denver. She did not like changes, especially big ones like this. She wondered how her sister could be so excited and happy at a time like this.

2. Point of view: _____

   Explanation: _____

   _____

   _____

MORE ABOUT POINT OF VIEW Work with a partner. Find selections in your book that use each point of view. Share your findings with a group.

© Hampton-Brown

LITERARY ANALYSIS: HYPERBOLE

Exaggerating for Effect

Hyperbole

Hyperbole is extreme exaggeration. Writers use hyperbole to make their writing more interesting. This airplane could win a race with a lightning bolt.

DIRECTIONS Read the passage. Underline each example of hyperbole. Then complete the chart.

> ## Ma and Pa
>
> My ma was so tall she could shove the clouds aside to give us a sunny day. My pa was so tiny he needed a stepladder to reach the kitchen counter. Auntie Jez's house covered forty acres. Whenever Ma and Pa visited Auntie Jez, they stayed a week because it took Pa two days to hike across the living room.

Hyperbole	What it Means
so tall she could	Ma was very

DIRECTIONS Make each statement humorous. Use hyperbole. Compare your hyperboles with a partner's.

1. **Statement:** He ran very fast.

   Hyperbole: _____

2. **Statement:** We made a lot of money.

   Hyperbole: _____

3. **Statement:** Rusty was a skinny dog.

   Hyperbole: _____

4. **Statement:** She sang very loudly.

   Hyperbole: _____

Stories About Flying

DIRECTIONS Underline the gerunds in the passage.

Working Together

Windrider and his son didn't know what to do. <u>Hauling</u> Dragonwings up the hill would require a wagon and a team of horses. Hiring those things would require money, and they had none. Moon Shadow went to town to call their friend, Miss Whitlaw, to stop her from visiting them the next day. After calling, he returned home.

The next day, Uncle and the rest of the Company showed up with a wagon. Uncle had been stubborn, but you didn't have to teach him about helping. The men lifted Dragonwings onto the wagon. Climbing the hill was hard work. Nonetheless, they continued pushing and pulling. In the end, they got the flying machine up the hill by moving it themselves. Windrider and Uncle liked to complain, but, in truth, they enjoyed working together.

Gerunds

A **gerund** is a verb form that ends in **–ing** and acts like a noun. A gerund can be the subject of the sentence or the object of a verb or preposition.

Flying is more than a dream.
We all love **flying**.
I dream about **flying**.

DIRECTIONS Complete each sentence with a gerund.

1. Windrider probably passed on his interest in _____flying_____ to his son.

2. One lesson of the story is to never stop _____.

3. I wonder if Laurence Yep enjoyed _____ *Dragonwings*.

4. _____ is one of my favorite pastimes.

5. My favorite form of exercise is _____.

6. In the summer, I enjoy _____.

7. In the winter, I enjoy _____.

8. If I go to college, I will probably have a lot of _____ to do.

MORE ABOUT GERUNDS Use gerunds in sentences about Moon Shadow, Windrider and Dragonwings. Choose gerunds from this list or choose some of your own: flying, dreaming, believing, hoping, working, succeeding, playing.

Themes For All

DIRECTIONS Follow the steps to compare "Windrider's Dream" and "The Dance."

1 **Make a Theme Log** Take notes and write a theme statement for "The Dance."

What the Story Says	What It Means

Theme

2 **Discuss Theme Statements** Meet with other students who have written similar theme statements. Discuss the details in the story that support your statements. Change your statements as necessary.

3 **Compare Themes** Study the information in the box. Review the theme statement for "Windrider's Dream." Then compare it with "The Dance." Discuss with your group whether the themes are universal, timeless, or both.

> **Universal and Timeless Themes**
>
> - A **universal** theme is one that all people can appreciate.
> - A **timeless** theme is one that can apply to any time period.
>   **Examples:**
>   The theme of honesty is both universal and timeless.
>   The theme of automobile safety is universal but not timeless.

4 **Write an Essay** On a separate sheet of paper, write an essay to compare the themes. Explain why the themes are universal, timeless or both.

Holding Onto a Dream

DIRECTIONS Work with a partner. Find the misplaced participial phrases. Rewrite each sentence.

> **Participial Phrases**
>
> A **participle** is a verb form that usually ends in –**ing** or –**ed**. A **participial phrase** begins with a participle. It acts like an adjective to describe a noun or pronoun. A participial phrase must be placed next to the word it describes.
>
> **Laughing scornfully,** Uncle criticized the dream.
>
> **Not:** Uncle criticized the dream **laughing scornfully.**

1. Father talked about his flying machine speaking matter-of-factly.

   Speaking matter-of-factly, Father talked

   about his flying machine.

2. Uncle urged Father to admit the truth snapping at his brother.

   _____

3. Uncle showed us to the door angered by Father's "nonsense."

   _____

4. I felt my Father, wrapped in his arm, was right.

   _____

5. We decided to hire a team of horses convinced Dragonwings would fly.

   _____

6. Black Dog demanded the money putting a knife to my throat.

   _____

7. Hand Clap bowed and greeted me, appearing as if by magic.

   _____

8. The Company trudged up the hill with food and coiled rope walking behind the wagon.

   _____

9. The motor carried Dragonwings toward the edge of the hillside coughing into life.

   _____

10. The Company watched Dragonwings soar above the fields holding their breath.

    _____

RESEARCH SKILLS

Using the Internet

DIRECTIONS Do a search for the Wright Brothers. Choose four Web sites. Follow the steps to evaluate the reliability of each site.

1 Write the address of the site.

2 Use the Rating Scale to rate the site. Write *1*, *2*, or *3* in each box.

3 Add the two ratings. Draw a star beside the most reliable sites to use for information about the Wright Brothers.

Web Site Reliability

The **reliability** of a Web site is how much you can trust the information it gives. A reliable Web site is usually one that:

- was created by an encyclopedia company, a college, a scientific organization, or a museum.

- cites other reliable sources, such as encyclopedias, textbooks, major news organizations, or experts.

Web Site Reliability Rating Scale

Reliability Rating	Type of Site (Who created the site?)	Sources Cited (What does the site refer to?)
1 = Low	an individual, interest group, or advertiser	no sources
2 = Medium	a government agency or business group	individual authors, independent researchers, or statements that cannot be verified
3 = High	an encyclopedia company, college, scientific organization, aquarium, or museum	encyclopedias, scientific journals, first-hand sources, recognized experts

Site 1: ___www.wright-brothers.org_____

[3] Type of Site + [3] Sources Cited = Total ___6___

Site 2: _____

[ ] Type of Site + [ ] Sources Cited = Total _____

Site 3: _____

[ ] Type of Site + [ ] Sources Cited = Total _____

Site 4: _____

[ ] Type of Site + [ ] Sources Cited = Total _____

DIRECTIONS Surfing the Internet, or looking for Web sites, can be fun. It is important, however, to protect yourself and your family. Answer the questions to show what you know about safety on the Internet.

1. What are two good reasons for surfing the Internet?

_____

2. Why is it important to be careful while surfing the Internet?

_____

3. What kinds of information should you never send over the Internet?

_____

4. Who can help you surf the Internet safely?

_____

DIRECTIONS Read the certificate. Check each item and sign the certificate, if you agree. You might want to copy it and put it near your computer.

Internet Safety Net

☐ If I am in a chatroom or on a Web site, I will **not**
  • give my real name.
  • give my address or phone number.
  • tell any information about my school.
  • tell any information about my family.

☐ I will not arrange to meet any on-line friends in person without talking to my parents or guardians first.

☐ I will not stay in a chatroom that uses bad language or makes me uncomfortable in any way.

☐ If I am not sure a Web site is right for me, I will
  • ask my parents, guardians, or a teacher to look at the site with me.
  • close the site if no adult is available.

_____   _____
Signature   Date

WRITING: A POEM

The Poet Within

DIRECTIONS Complete the chart to plan your poem. Review the definitions of literary devices on pages 470–476 in your book. Use the ideas in the chart to write your poem.

Literary Device

Writers use **literary devices** to create a specific effect. There are many types of literary devices, including:

alliteration	personification	rhyme
consonance	onomatopoeia	metaphor
assonance	repetition	simile

	Example	Your Ideas
1. Decide what message you want to share.	Nature is precious and beautiful in winter.	
2. Make a list of images and details you want to include in your poem.	fox the color of flame from a fire heavy snow falling feel isolated is cold and quiet	
3. Use literary devices to help readers "picture" your message. Include at least one metaphor or simile.	Alliteration: showers of silent, shifting snow Consonance: they gently fall upon the hill Metaphor: the fox is a flame Personification: it dances across the snow Simile: like tiny balls of cotton	

The Short Form

DIRECTIONS Read the passage Jodhi wrote. Underline the most important words and phrases. Then compress the deep emotions or important ideas into a few words.

> **Compression in Poetry**
>
> Poets often use just a few words to express deep thoughts, feelings, and ideas. They **compress** their language by choosing only the most important words. Then they add similes and metaphors to create poetry.

Jodhi's Thoughts	Jodhi's Dream
There are <u>so many things</u> I want <u>to do</u>. I want to travel and see all the wonderful sights in the whole world. Someday I want to live in many different places and learn to speak all the languages, so everyone will understand me. Then I want to stop suffering and make sure every person has a home and food and a job. Now is the time to start preparing for all the things I think are so important. I'll study in school and help people as much as I can. Right now is the time to start making a difference for others, and begin living the life I want.	So many things to do

DIRECTIONS Create a poem. Add similes and metaphors to the compressed language.

So many things to do.

The world is a meal with many dishes.

_____   _____

_____   _____

_____   _____

_____   _____

MORE ABOUT COMPRESSION IN POETRY Write a paragraph about a topic that you care about. Then compress the language and add similes and metaphors to create a poem.

Acknowledgments

Every effort has been made to secure permission, but if any omissions have been made, please let us know. We gratefully acknowledge the following permissions:

p 14, Text excerpts from LIVES OF THE MUSICIANS, text copyright © 1993 by Kathleen Krull; used with permission of Harcourt, Inc.

p 37, Excerpted from THE WORLD BOOK ENCYCLOPEDIA. © 1998 World Book, Inc. By permission of the publisher. www.worldbook.com

p 46, Readers' Guide to Periodical Literature. Vol. 100, No.6, August 2000, p.721. Copyright © 2000 H.W. Wilson Company. Material reprinted with permission of H.W. Wilson.

p 51, Excerpted from Space Exploration by Carole Stott. Text copyright © 1997 Dorling Kindersley Limited, reproduced by permission.

p 51, "User Friendly" by T. Ernesto Bethancourt, copyright © 1989 by T. Ernesto Bethancourt, from CONNECTIONS: SHORT STORIES by Donald R. Gallo, Editor. Used by permission of Dell Publishing, a division of Random House, Inc.

p 133, Readers' Guide to Periodical Literature, March 1959–February 1961, p. 350. Copyright © 1961 H. W. Wilson Company. Material reprinted with permission of H.W. Wilson.

p 154, "Echoes of the Past Linger on Joad's Road" by Kelly Kurt, excerpted with permission of the Associated Press.

Photographs:

Artville: p 140 (sub sandwich), p 140 (pancakes)

Aurora & Quantum Productions: p 115 (Aimee Mullins, © Lynn Johnson / Aurora)

Judi L. Baker:. p 6 (Balinese puppet, © Judi L. Baker)

Janette Beckman: p 66 (kids singing)

CORBIS: p 33 (rapids, © Phil Schermeister), p 78 (café, © Richard Bickel), p 80 (Christopher Reeve, © John Marshall-Mantel), p 94 (bazaar, © Wolfgang Kaehler), p 119 (Kabuki, © Charles and Josette Lenars), p 128 (Melba Patillo, © Corbis/Bettman Archive), p 144 (boy in Dust Bowl, © Corbis/Bettman Archive), p 139 (Migrant Mother, © Corbis)

Corel: p 63 (Capital Building)

Digital Stock: p 89 (UN headquarters)

Harcourt, Inc.: pp 72, 74 (Illustration from AMISTAD RISING, by Veronica Chambers, illustrations copyright © 1998 by Paul Lee, used with permission of Harcourt, Inc.)

Hulton / Archive:: p 68 (women's suffrage, © Paul Thompson), p 71 (Lewis Tappan, © Hulton/Archive), p 146 (soupline, © Hulton/Archive)

Lee and Low Books: p 122 (Illustrations copyright © by Dom Lee)

Craig Lovell: p 20 (Budapest Hungary)

Garaham McIndoe: p 112 (Aimee Mullins)

NASA: p 41 (Space Station, © 1997 Dorling Kindersley Limited)

PhotoDisc: p140 (paper bag)

PhotoEdit: p 82 (peer mediation group, © Mary Kate Denny), p 119 (sumo wrestlers, © Tom McCarthy), p 140 (soda bottle, © Michael Newman), p 159 (girl helping grandmother, © David Young Wolff)

Pictor: p 19 (kids around computer, © John Davis)

R.C. Gorman's Navajo Gallery: p 13 (Navajo Return, © Courtesy of R.C. Gorman's Navajo Gallery)

Patrick Tregenza: p 81 (Katrina and Jose)

The Stock Market: p 116 (flood, © Phillip Wallick), p 119 (bullet train, © Photowood, Inc.)

Superstock: p 118 (Rosie the Riveter, © Superstock)

Stone: p 61 (Liberty Bell, © Reza Estakhrian), p 119 (temple, © Gavin Hellier), p119 (sushi, © Chris Everard)

Walker Art Center: p 2 (TV Cello by Nam Jun Paik, © Collection Walker At Center, Minneapolis. Formerly the collection of Otto Piene and Elizabeth Goldring, Massachusetts collection. Walker Art Center. T.B. Walker Acquisition Fund 1992), p 17 (Spoonbridge and Cherry, © Collection Walker Art Center, Minneapolis Gift of Frederick R. Wisman in honor of his parents, William and Mary Weisman 1988)

Illustrations:

Paul Bachem: p 35

Marcia Bateman: pp 22, 28, 35, 84, 85

Matthew Brown: p 18

Chi Chung: p 167

Len Epstein: pp 26, 31, 40, 48, 53, 54

Morissa Gellar: pp 4, 5, 18

Judy Love: pp 25, 27, 48, 54, 58, 70, 87, 99, 102, 103, 110, 129, 138, 141, 155, 160, 165, 166

Russel Nemec: pp 15, 34, 36, 38, 75, 89, 97, 123

John Ward: p 51, 163

Hampton-Brown Staff Credits

Editorial Staff: Susan Blackaby, Kellie Crain, Phyllis Edwards, Suzanne Gardner, Fredrick Ignacio, Barbara Linde, Dawn Liseth, Daphne Liu, Sheron Long, Michele McFadden, Elizabeth Sengel, Sharon Ursino, Andreya Valabek, Lynn Yokoe

Design and Production Staff: Marcia Bateman Walker, Matthew Brown, Andrea Carter, Connie DeLa Garza, Lauren Grace, Davis Hernandez, Russell Nemec, Debbie Saxton, Curtis Spitler, Margaret Tisdale, JR Walker

Permissions Staff: Barbara Mathewson